London 2012
National Venues Atlas and Guide

Route Planning maps

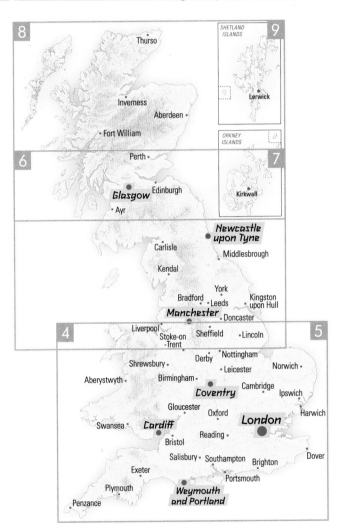

Geographers' A-Z Map Company Ltd.

Fairfield Road, Borough Green, Sevenoaks, Kent TN15 8PP
Telephone: 01732 781000 (Enquiries & Trade Sales)
01732 783422 (Retail Sales)

Edition 1 2012

© Copyright of Geographers' A-Z Map Company Limited

QR codes throughout this book can be scanned
with free mobile device apps for the latest information

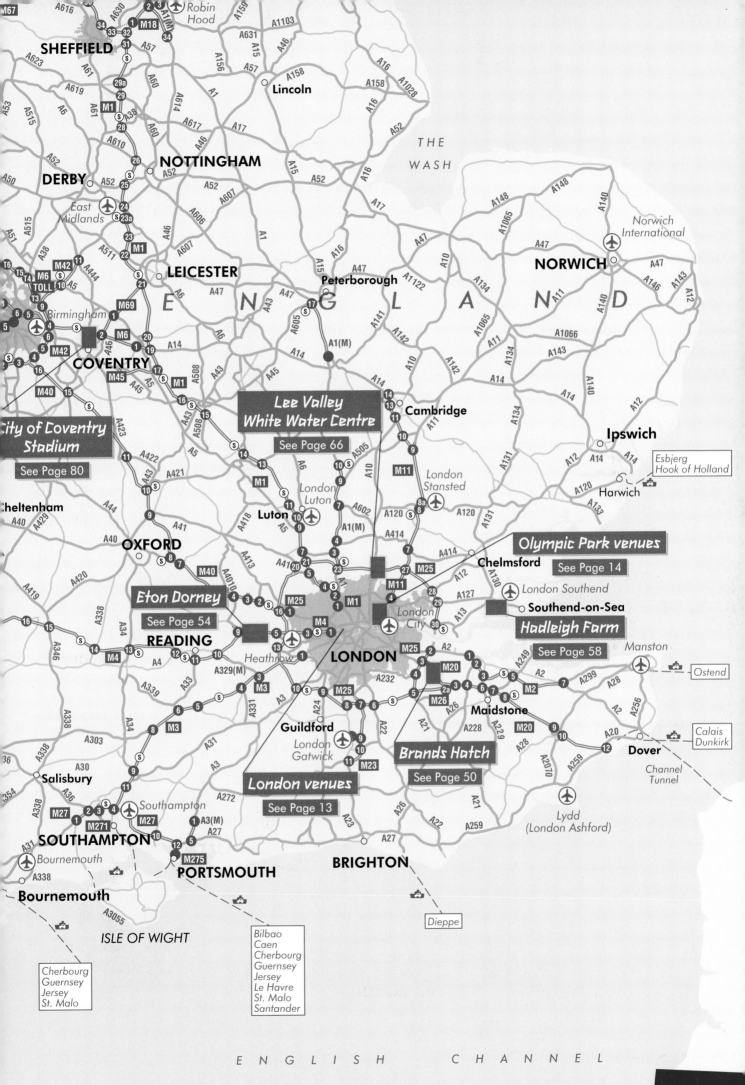

SHEFFIELD
Robin Hood
Lincoln
DERBY
NOTTINGHAM
East Midlands
LEICESTER
Peterborough
NORWICH
Norwich International
E N G L A N D
Birmingham
COVENTRY
City of Coventry Stadium
See Page 80
Cheltenham
Cambridge
Ipswich
Esbjerg Hook of Holland
Lee Valley White Water Centre
See Page 66
Harwich
OXFORD
London Luton
Luton
London Stansted
Olympic Park venues
See Page 14
Chelmsford
London Southend
Southend-on-Sea
Eton Dorney
See Page 54
READING
Heathrow
LONDON
Hadleigh Farm
See Page 58
Manston
Ostend
London City
Guildford
London Gatwick
Brands Hatch
See Page 50
Maidstone
Dover
Calais Dunkirk
London venues
See Page 13
Channel Tunnel
Salisbury
Lydd (London Ashford)
Southampton
SOUTHAMPTON
Bournemouth
PORTSMOUTH
BRIGHTON
Bournemouth
ISLE OF WIGHT
Dieppe

Cherbourg
Guernsey
Jersey
St. Malo

Bilbao
Caen
Cherbourg
Guernsey
Jersey
Le Havre
St. Malo
Santander

THE WASH

E N G L I S H   C H A N N E L

5

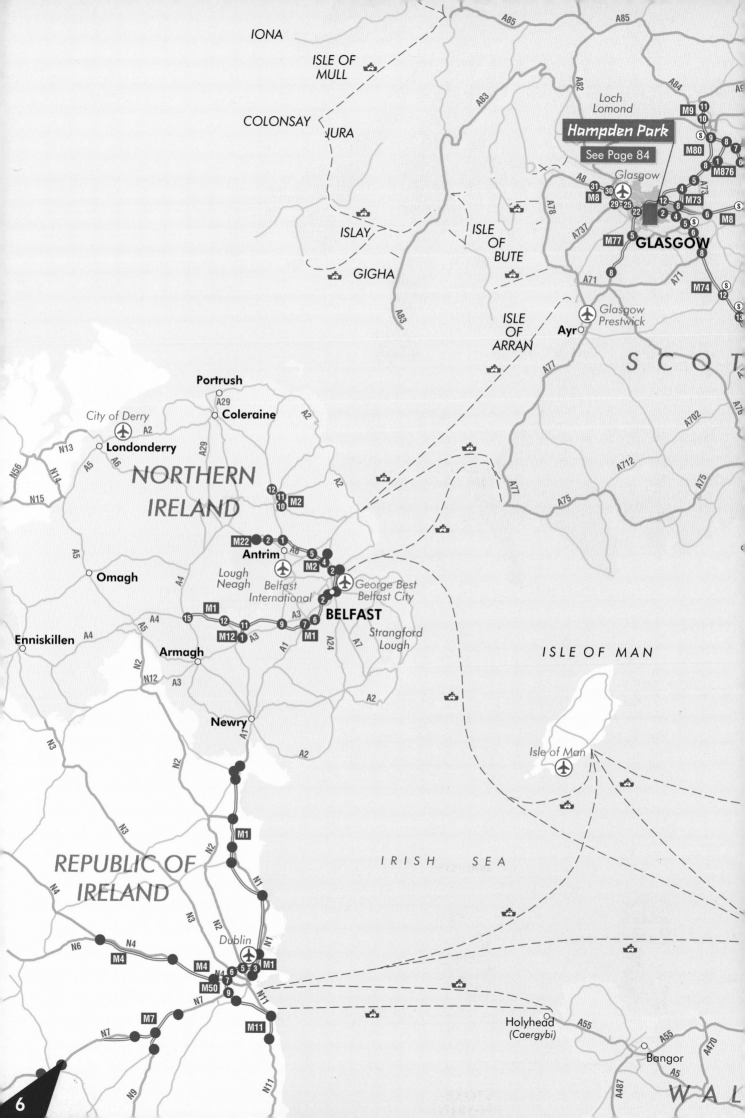

IONA

ISLE OF MULL

COLONSAY

JURA

ISLAY

GIGHA

ISLE OF BUTE

ISLE OF ARRAN

Loch Lomond

Hampden Park

See Page 84

Glasgow

GLASGOW

Glasgow Prestwick

Ayr

S C O T

Portrush

City of Derry

Coleraine

Londonderry

NORTHERN IRELAND

Omagh

Antrim

Lough Neagh

Belfast International

George Best Belfast City

BELFAST

Strangford Lough

Enniskillen

Armagh

Newry

REPUBLIC OF IRELAND

Dublin

ISLE OF MAN

Isle of Man

I R I S H   S E A

Holyhead (Caergybi)

Bangor

W A L

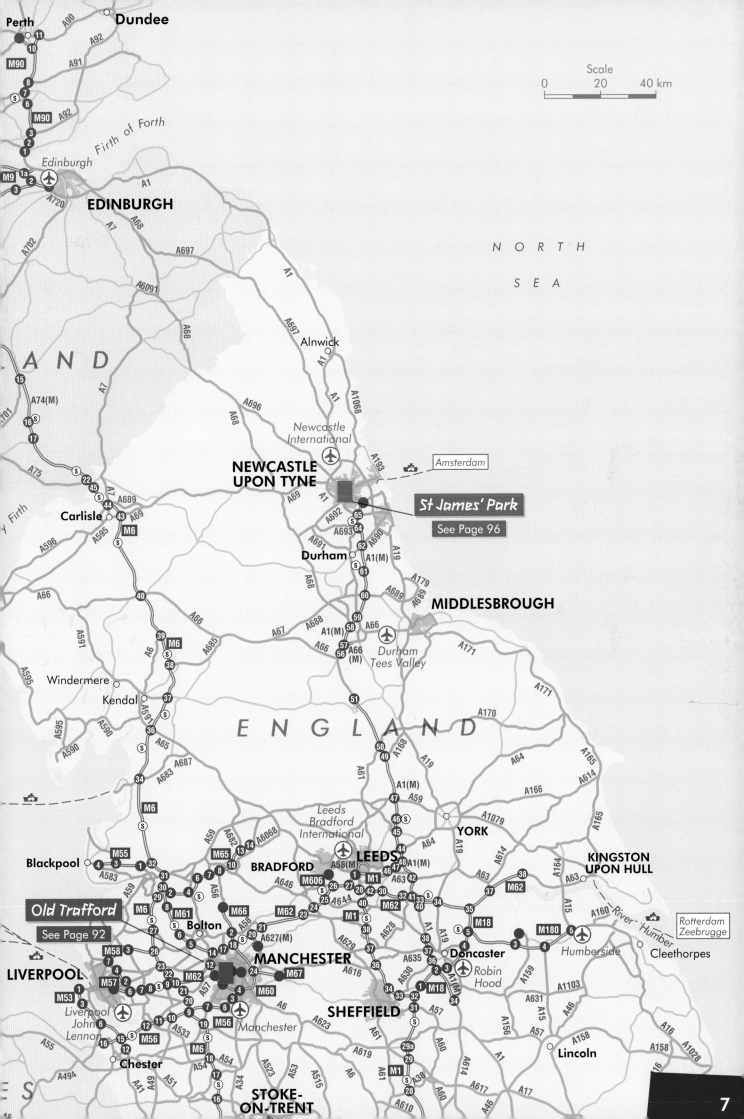

St James' Park
See Page 96

Old Trafford
See Page 92

Amsterdam

Rotterdam
Zeebrugge

NORTH SEA

ENGLAND

Perth
Dundee
EDINBURGH
Edinburgh
Firth of Forth
Alnwick
Newcastle International
NEWCASTLE UPON TYNE
Durham
MIDDLESBROUGH
Durham Tees Valley
Carlisle
Windermere
Kendal
Blackpool
Leeds Bradford International
BRADFORD
LEEDS
YORK
KINGSTON UPON HULL
Humberside
Cleethorpes
River Humber
Bolton
Old Trafford
LIVERPOOL
MANCHESTER
Liverpool John Lennon
Manchester
Doncaster
Robin Hood
SHEFFIELD
Chester
STOKE-ON-TRENT
Lincoln

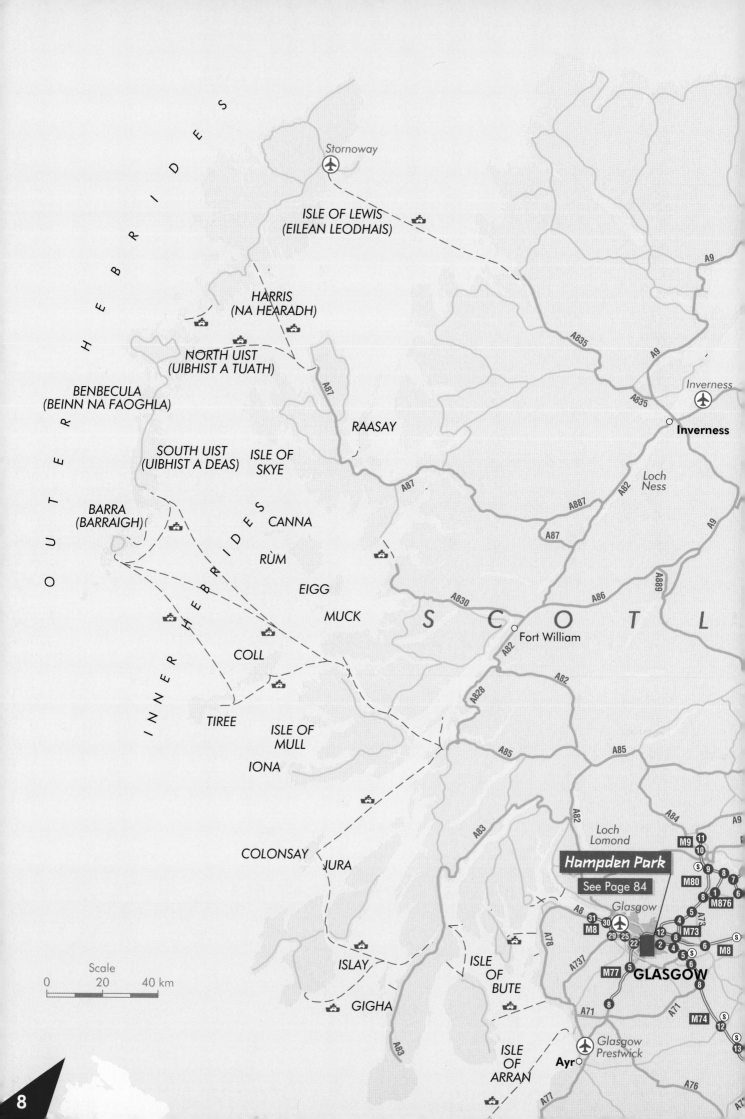

OUTER HEBRIDES

Stornoway

ISLE OF LEWIS
(EILEAN LEODHAIS)

HARRIS
(NA HEARADH)

NORTH UIST
(UIBHIST A TUATH)

BENBECULA
(BEINN NA FAOGHLA)

RAASAY

SOUTH UIST
(UIBHIST A DEAS)

ISLE OF
SKYE

BARRA
(BARRAIGH)

CANNA

RÙM

EIGG

INNER HEBRIDES

MUCK

COLL

TIREE

ISLE OF
MULL

IONA

COLONSAY

JURA

ISLAY

GIGHA

ISLE
OF
BUTE

ISLE
OF
ARRAN

S C O T L

Inverness

Inverness

Loch
Ness

Fort William

Loch
Lomond

Hampden Park
See Page 84

Glasgow

GLASGOW

Glasgow
Prestwick

Ayr

A9
A835
A9
A835
A887
A82
A87
A87
A9
A889
A86
A830
A82
A828
A82
A85
A85
A83
A82
A84
A9
A8
A78
A737
A71
A71
A76
A77
A83

M9 11
10
9 8 7
M80
S
8 1 6
M876
5
4 A73
M8 31 30
29 25 22
12 M73
2 4
3 6
M8
M77
6
8
M74 12
13

Scale
0   20   40 km

8

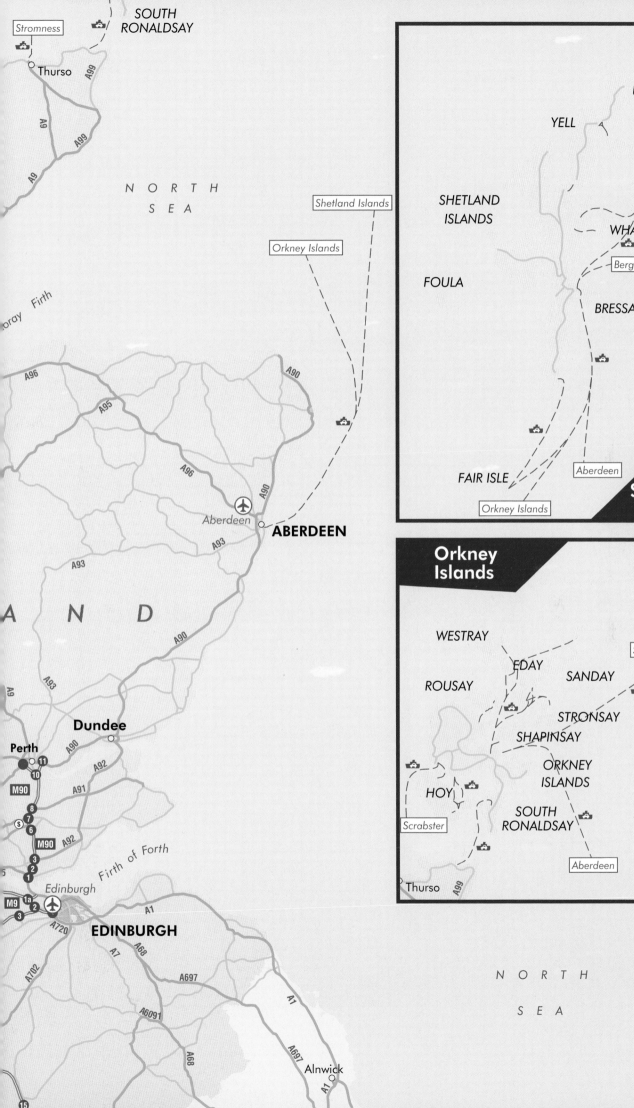

London Connections

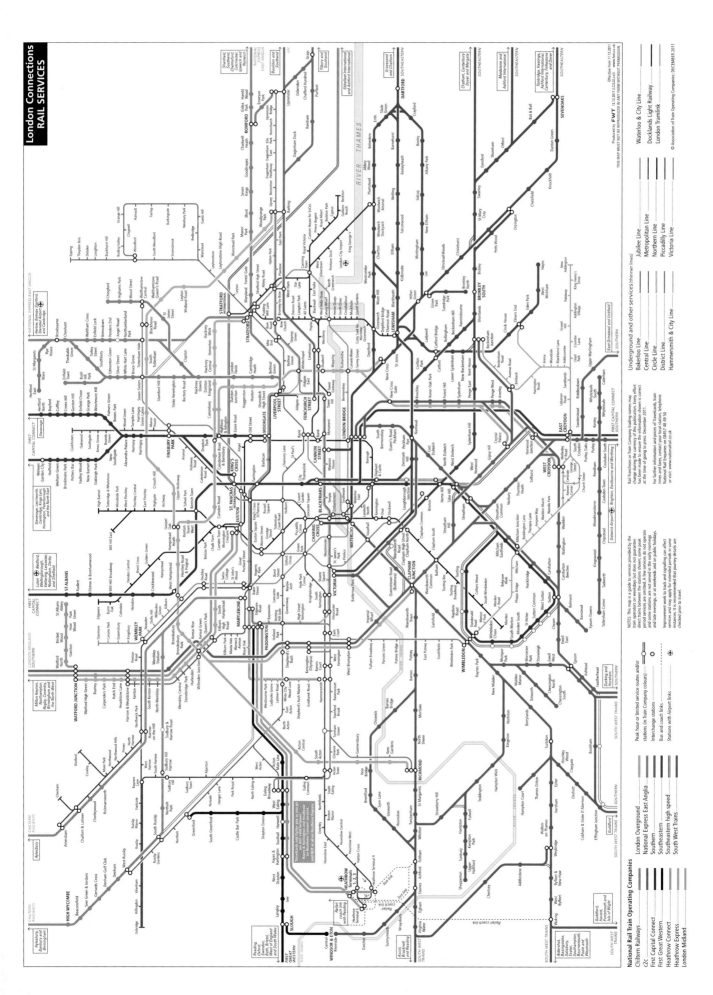

London Connections
RAIL SERVICES

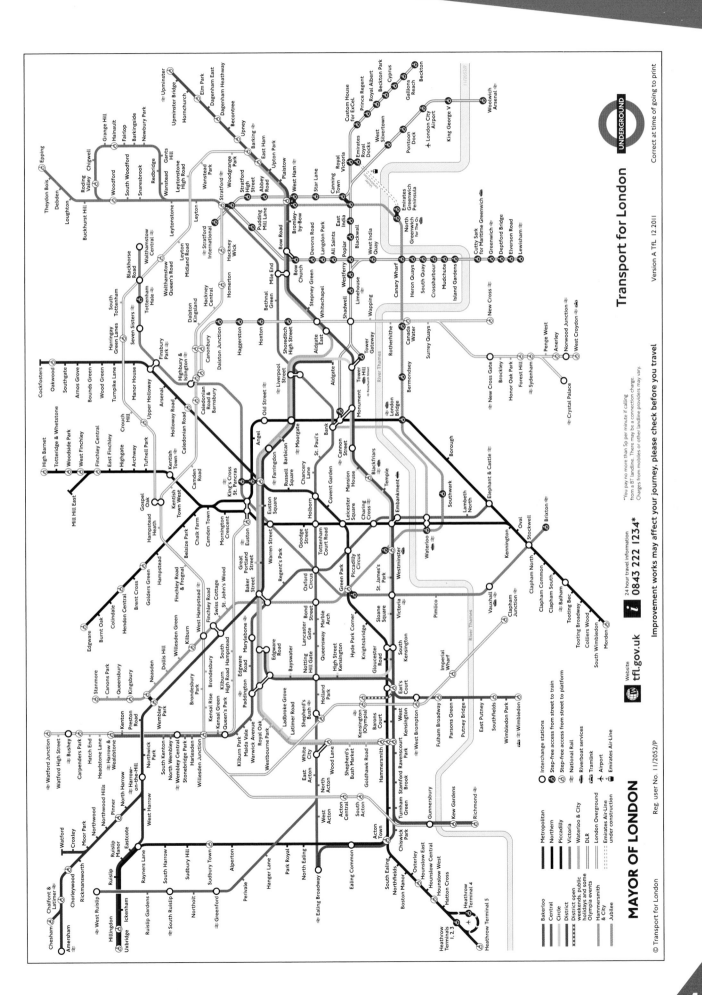

Games travel information

scan for www.london2012.com/getting-to-the-games

London 2012 is aiming for a 'public transport' Games, there will be no parking at or near any venue. You can travel to each venue using different types of public transport, or by walking or cycling.

Transport information is accurate at the date of publication but may be subject to change. Spectators are advised to visit the London 2012 website for the latest information.

Venues in London

London's transport system will be very busy, so you should allow plenty of time to travel to, from and between venues. Check the information on travelling to your event to find out where your venue is, the best way to get there and how long your journey will take between the recommended stations serving venues. London is well-served by public transport with travel options including the London Underground, London Overground, Docklands Light Railway, National Rail, buses and river services.

Travel Tickets

London 2012 ticket holders can benefit from a range of special travel tickets for the Games. Spectators with a ticket for a Games event in London will receive a one-day Games Travelcard for the day of that event valid within zones 1 to 9. This includes London Underground (Tube), London Overground, Docklands Light Railway (DLR), buses, trams and National Rail services, including the Javelin® service between St Pancras International and Stratford International stations, but excluding the Heathrow, Stansted or Gatwick Express trains, or taxis and private hire vehicles. Spectators will be entitled to a one-third discount on the price of London 2012 River service tickets.

2012 Games spectator journey planner

Plan your journey using the 2012 Games spectator journey planner. It will provide you with:
- Estimated journey times to and from Games venues from anywhere in Great Britain.
- Estimated walking and cycling time to and from recommended stations to Games venues.
- Timetable information to allow Games ticket holders to plan their travel.
- Links to travel booking sites to enable Games ticket holders to purchase travel tickets in advance of travel.
- Recommended routes to make your journey as easy as possible.

Rail

The National Rail network connects London and all the co-Host Cities for the London 2012 venues. Extra Rail services will be provided to Games venues, and trains will run later from London to key destinations up to approximately two hours away, such as Birmingham, Manchester, Leeds and Cardiff.

Shuttle Buses

Shuttle buses will be provided from some recommended stations to London 2012 and co-Host City venues, particularly where these stations are more than a short walk away from the venue entrance. These shuttles will be low-floor accessible buses and the service will be available for all spectators.

2012 Games park-and-ride [P+R]

- Secure park-and-ride sites with limited space will be provided at convenient locations.
- Park-and-ride services must be booked in advance.
- Venues with park-and-ride facilities during the Olympic Games include: the Olympic Park, ExCeL, Greenwich Park (30 July only), Eton Dorney, Hadleigh Farm, the Lee Valley White Water Centre and Weymouth and Portland.
- Venues with park-and-ride facilities during the Paralympic Games include: the Olympic Park, ExCeL, and Eton Dorney.

Blue Badge Parking

Blue Badge Parking spaces are available for spectators who hold a valid Blue Badge or recognised national disability permit.
- Blue Badge Parking spaces must be booked in advance.

2012 Games coach services

- During the Olympic Games coach services will be provided to the Olympic Park, ExCeL, Greenwich Park (30 July only) and Weymouth and Portland from a range of locations outside the M25. Coaches will pick up from bus stops and bus stations throughout Great Britain.
- During the Paralympic Games, 2012 Games coach services will be provided to the Olympic Park and ExCeL
- All passengers on the coach services will have a dedicated seat or wheelchair space.
- All seats and wheelchair spaces on 2012 Games coach services must be booked in advance:

scan for www.firstgroupgamestravel.com

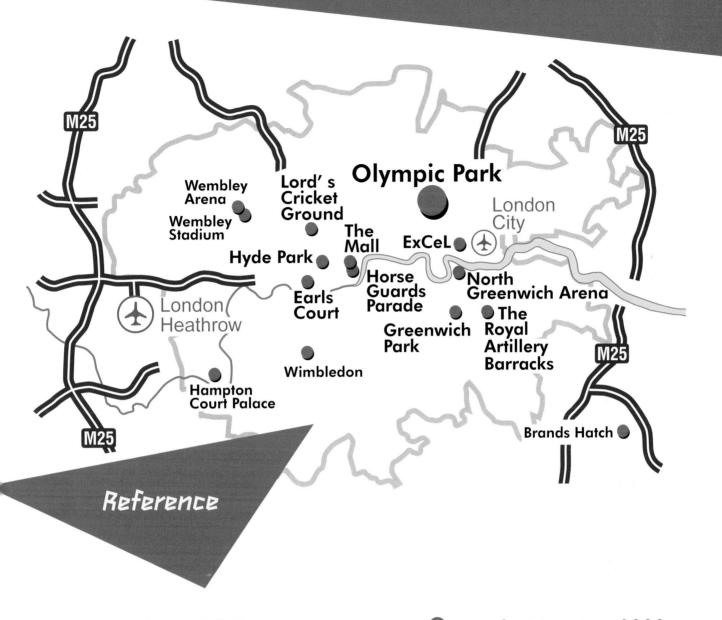

Olympic Park

London City

Wembley Arena
Wembley Stadium
Lord's Cricket Ground
The Mall
ExCeL
Hyde Park
Horse Guards Parade
North Greenwich Arena
Earls Court
Greenwich Park
The Royal Artillery Barracks
London Heathrow
Wimbledon
Hampton Court Palace
Brands Hatch

M25

Reference

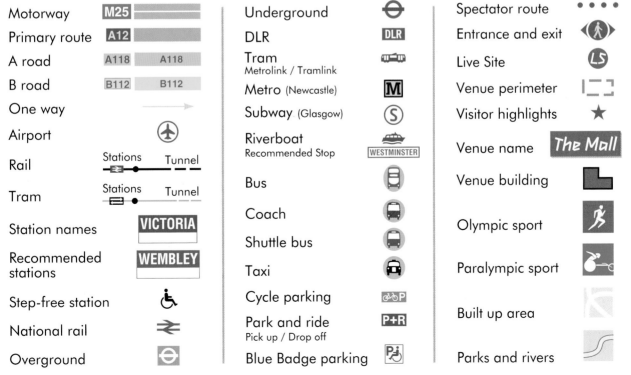

Motorway	M25	
Primary route	A12	
A road	A118	A118
B road	B112	B112
One way		
Airport	✈	
Rail	Stations — Tunnel	
Tram	Stations — Tunnel	
Station names	VICTORIA	
Recommended stations	WEMBLEY	
Step-free station	♿	
National rail	⇌	
Overground	Ⓞ	

Underground	⊖
DLR	DLR
Tram (Metrolink / Tramlink)	🚋
Metro (Newcastle)	Ⓜ
Subway (Glasgow)	Ⓢ
Riverboat (Recommended Stop)	WESTMINSTER
Bus	🚌
Coach	🚌
Shuttle bus	🚌
Taxi	🚕
Cycle parking	🚲P
Park and ride (Pick up / Drop off)	P+R
Blue Badge parking	♿P

Spectator route	• • • •
Entrance and exit	👁
Live Site	LS
Venue perimeter	⌐ ┐
Visitor highlights	★
Venue name	The Mall
Venue building	⬛
Olympic sport	🏃
Paralympic sport	♿
Built up area	
Parks and rivers	

Olympic Park

27 July – 12 August

29 August – 9 September

The Olympic Park is a 2.5 sq km site in Stratford, east London, providing a purpose-built and easily accessible centre stage for the Games.

The Park includes nine sporting venues.

Travelling to Stratford

 London City Airport is just 4kms from the Olympic Park venue in Stratford. Passengers travelling to and from the airport enjoy fast transfers on the Docklands Light Railway (DLR). For general airport enquiries please call +44 (0)20 7646 0088.

 There are three National Rail stations providing access to the Olympic Park: Stratford station, with direct train services from London and East Anglia; Stratford International station, with direct train services from London, Ebbsfleet and Kent; and, West Ham station, with direct train services from London and Essex.

National Rail services will run from London Liverpool Street to Stratford. If you are travelling from the north into London King's Cross, London St. Pancras or London Euston stations, use the Javelin® service to Stratford International from London St. Pancras International. The Javelin® service will also run from Ebbsfleet in Kent.

♿ Accessibility

London City Airport welcomes passengers with reduced mobility or special requirements.

Stratford, Stratford International and West Ham stations are all step-free with staff assistance available. It is recommended that people with accessibility needs use Stratford and Stratford International, as West Ham station is approximately 1.6km from the venue's entrance.

LS London 2012 Live Site, Victoria Park.

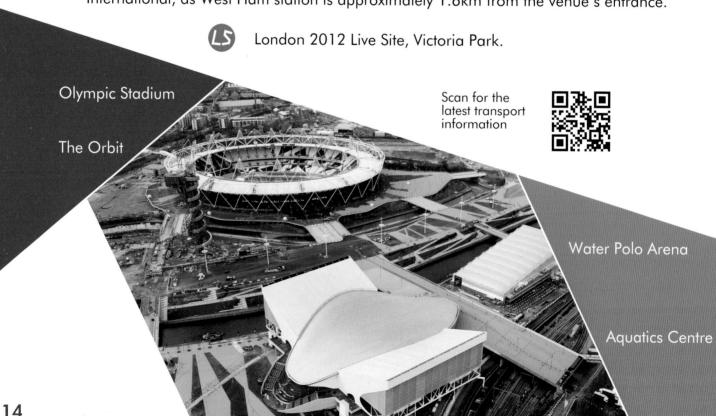

Olympic Stadium

The Orbit

Scan for the latest transport information

Water Polo Arena

Aquatics Centre

Olympic Park

27 July - 12 August

29 August - 9 September

Getting to the Venue

There are two recommended London Underground stations providing access to the Olympic Park: Stratford, on the Jubilee and Central lines, and West Ham on the District, Hammersmith & City and Jubilee lines. West Ham station is approximately 15 minutes walk from the Greenway Gate entrance to the Olympic Park along a dedicated walkway.

DLR The Olympic Park is served by the two lines of the Docklands Light Railway (DLR), with stops at Stratford, Stratford International and West Ham stations. The DLR runs to Stratford from Lewisham and Woolwich Arsenal stations in south-east London. From central London, get the DLR from Tower Gateway and change at Poplar.

The North London Line on London Overground connects Richmond to Stratford and avoids central London. If travelling from south London, use the East London Line and change at Canonbury on to the North London Line to Stratford.

The Olympic Park cannot be accessed by Thames river services as it is not located on the River Thames. However, there will be a limited-capacity canal boat passenger service departing from Limehouse Basin or Tottenham Hale to Old Ford Lock (Victoria Gate entrance) and Homerton Road (Eton Manor Gate entrance). While not a quick travel option, it is an interesting alternative. Due to limited capacity on boats, pre-booking is recommended.

London has an extensive bus network and there are routes and stops in the area. London's buses have low floors and provide audio and visual information.
There is one wheelchair space per bus.

There will be 2012 Games coach services to the Olympic Park from a range of locations. Services are planned to arrive at the venue for the start of sessions.

The transport network to the Olympic Park will be extremely busy, so while it is best to plan your journey in advance, remember to check for any last minute changes before you travel.

wenlock

Having travelled 8,000 miles across the UK, the Olympic Flame arrives at the Olympic Stadium for the Opening Ceremony on 27 July.

Limited, pre-booked parking will be provided for disabled spectators who are UK Blue Badge holders or members of an equivalent national scheme.

 Regular park-and-ride shuttle-bus services will run directly to the Olympic Park from Hertfordshire County Showground to the Eton Manor Transport Hub and from Lakeside Shopping Centre to the Greenway Transport Hub.

Park-and-rail services are available from Ebbsfleet International station where trains run directly to Stratford International and the Olympic Park.

 There are six 'greenway' walking routes that connect with the Olympic Park: Lea Valley North, Hackney Parks, Victoria Park and Stepney, Limehouse Cut, Epping Forest and the Elevated Greenway.

The walking routes from the venue's transport malls are step-free.

 Taxi and private hire vehicle drop-off areas will be provided at the Eton Manor Transport Hub and the Greenway Transport Hub.

 Greenway cycling routes to the Olympic Park include Lee Valley North, Hackney Parks, Victoria Park and Stepney, Limehouse Cut, Epping Forest and the Elevated Greenway. Free, secure, managed cycle parking will be provided at the Eton Manor Transport Hub, the Greenway Transport Hub and Victoria Park.

• • • • Recommended spectator access routes to and from the venue.

 Venue entrance or exit.

 London 2012 Live Site. Park Live East and Park Live West, Olympic Park.

Scan for the latest transport information

Olympic Park
Pull out map

mandeville™

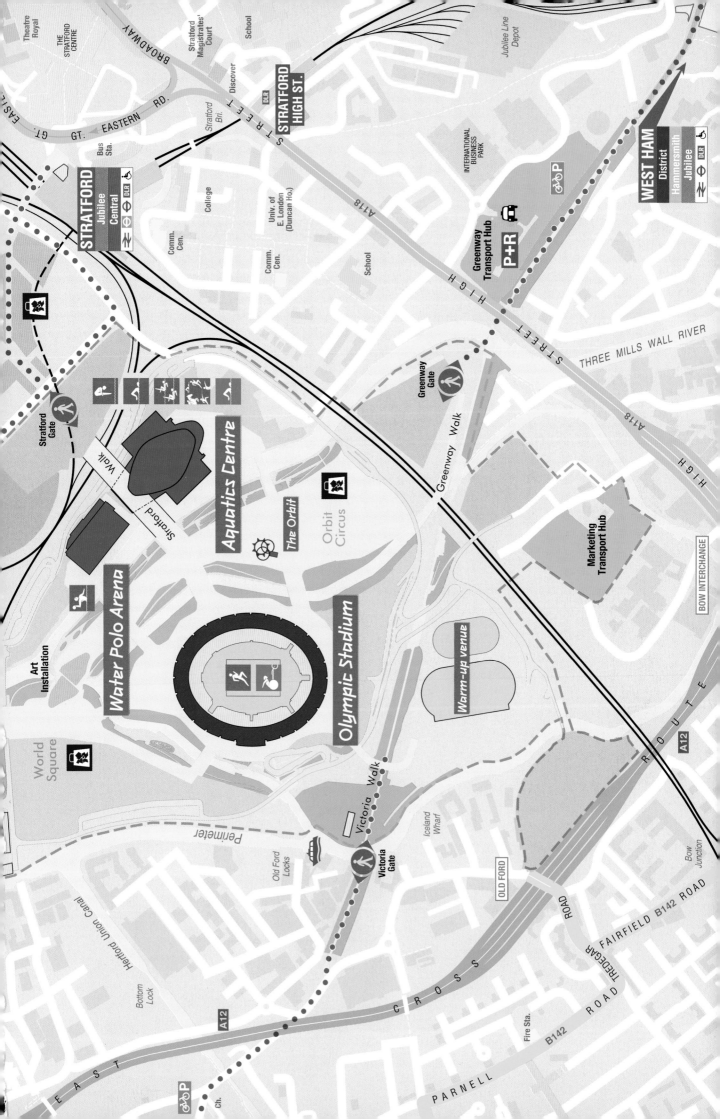

Olympic Park Map

Olympic sport

Paralympic sport

Venue entrance

Spectator route

Step-Free Station

London 2012 shop

0   100 m

LEYTON MILLS

HIGH   A112   ROAD

LEYTON   MAJOR

ROAD   ANGEL

A112

CHOBHAM ROAD

LEYTON

ROAD

A12

Nursery Ed. Cen.

Comm. Cen.

Sch.

St. Paul's Ch.

Stratford Picture Ho.

LANE

RD.

A118

High Speed 1

STRATFORD INTERNATIONAL

DLR

Bus Sta.

WESTFIELD STRATFORD CITY SHOPPING CENTRE

Hospitality Centre

LEYTON MILLS

Perimeter

Athletes Transport Hub

Eton Manor

BMX Track

Olympic and Paralympic Village

A106   ROAD

Eton   Manor   Walk

Eton Manor Gate

RUCKHOLT   ROAD

Velodrome

The Street Market

Basketball Arena

Wetlands Walk

Way

Eton Manor Transport Hub

P+R

P

RIVER   LEA

Temple Mills Bridge

ROUTE

LEA INTERCHANGE

River Lawns

Park Live East

London

Riverbank Arena

Warm-up venue

EAST   CROSS   A106   W   A12

Britannia Row

Park Live West

LS

Copper Box

HOMERTON   B112

HACKNEY MARSH RECREATION GROUND

WICK WOODLAND HACKNEY MARSH

Gainsborough Rd. Bri.

International Broadcast Centre

Main Press Centre

School

HACKNEY WICK

Copper Box

The Copper Box will be the venue for Handball, Goalball and the Fencing discipline of Modern Pentathlon during the London 2012 Games.

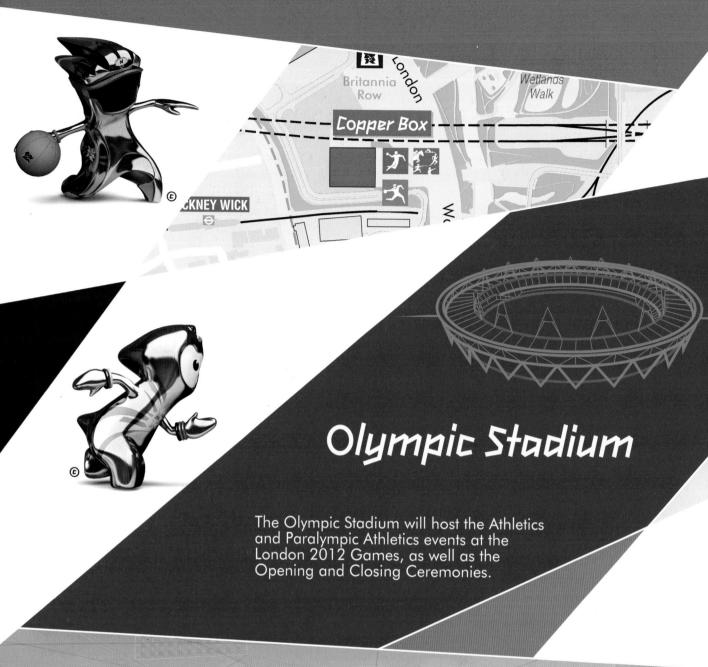

Olympic Stadium

The Olympic Stadium will host the Athletics and Paralympic Athletics events at the London 2012 Games, as well as the Opening and Closing Ceremonies.

Water Polo Arena

The Water Polo Arena will host both the men's and women's Water Polo competitions during the Olympic Games. It will contain a warm-up pool and a competition pool.

Water Polo Arena

Walk

Stratford

Aquatics Centre

The Orbit

Olympic Stadium

Victoria Walk

Victoria Gate

Aquatics Centre

During the London 2012 Games, the Aquatics Centre will be the venue for Swimming, Paralympic Swimming, Diving, Synchronised Swimming and the swimming element of the Modern Pentathlon.

Eton Manor

The sporting facilities at Eton Manor will be the venue for Wheelchair Tennis during the London 2012 Games.

Riverbank Arena

The temporary Riverbank Arena located in the Olympic Park will have two separate pitches, one with spectator seating. The facility will be used for Olympic Hockey and Paralympic 5-a-side and 7-a-side Football.

Riverbank Arena

Warm-up venue

Velodrome

During the London 2012 Games, the Velodrome will host Track Cycling and Paralympic Track Cycling.

BMX Track

The 400-metre circuit is located next to the Velodrome in the north of the Olympic Park.

Eton Manor

BMX Track

Athletes Transport Hub

Velodrome

The Street Market

Park Live East

Basketball Arena

Manor Walk

Basketball Arena

During the London 2012 Games, the Basketball Arena will host Basketball, Wheelchair Basketball, Wheelchair Rugby and the final stages of the Handball competition.

Earls Court first opened its doors in 1937.

During the Games, it will have a capacity of 15,000 for the Volleyball competition.

Getting to the Venue

 Earl's Court is the recommended London Underground station for this venue. The Piccadilly line runs to the venue from central London, London Heathrow Airport and north-west London. The District line serves the venue from central London, Paddington, Wimbledon, Ealing Broadway and Richmond.

 West London Line services run to West Brompton station from Milton Keynes, Clapham Junction and Willesden Junction. However, there is only a limited service to and from this station.

 London has an extensive bus network and there are routes and stops in the area.

Limited, pre-booked parking will be provided for disabled spectators who are UK Blue Badge holders or members of an equivalent national scheme.

 Earls Court is easily accessible on foot from local residential areas and the venue is only a short walk from Earl's Court station.

 There will be a taxi and private hire vehicle pick up/drop-off point close to the venue.

 Free, secure, managed cycle parking will be provided at the venue.

 Recommended spectator access routes to and from the venue.

 Venue entrance or exit.

Scan for the latest transport information

Volleyball

The first Olympic Volleyball competition was held in 1964, when the gold medals were won by the Soviet Union (men) and Japan (women).

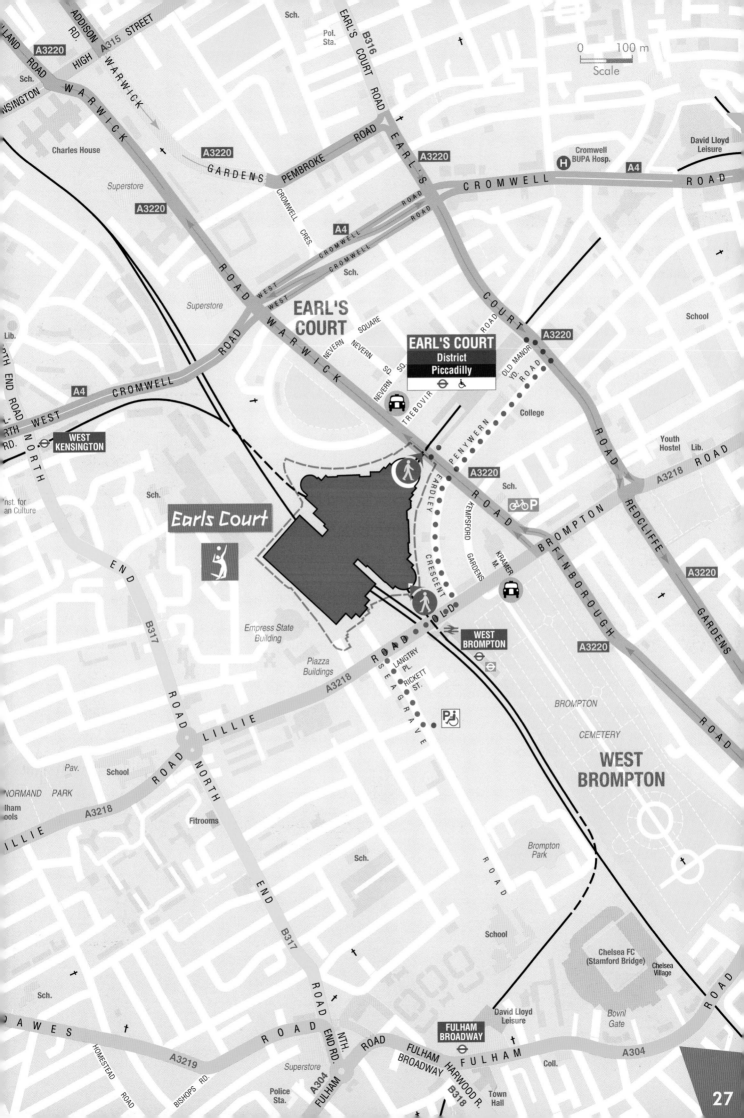

LAND ROAD
A3220

ADDISON RD.
A315 STREET
HIGH

Sch.
Pol. Sta.
EARL'S COURT ROAD
B316
†

WARWICK
GARDENS
PEMBROKE ROAD
A3220

Charles House
Superstore
A3220

†

A4
CROMWELL CRES.
CROMWELL ROAD
A3220
CROMWELL ROAD
A4
EARL'S ROAD

Cromwell BUPA Hosp.
H
A4
David Lloyd Leisure

CROMWELL ROAD
A3220

West A3220 Road
Superstore
CROMWELL ROAD
Sch.

EARL'S COURT

School

WARWICK ROAD
NEVERN SQUARE
NEVERN SQ.
NEVERN SQ.
†

EARL'S COURT
District
Piccadilly

Lib.

A4 CROMWELL

WEST
KENSINGTON

COURT ROAD
OLD MANOR YD.
A3220
†
College

'nst. for
an Culture

Sch.
TREBOVIR
†

Earls Court

PENYWERN ROAD
A3220
Sch.

Youth Hostel
Lib.
A3218 ROAD

EARDLEY CRESCENT
KEMPSFORD GARDENS
KRAMER M.
BROMPTON ROAD

B
P

REDCLIFFE ROAD
A3220

END B317 ROAD

Empress State Building
Piazza Buildings
A3218 ROAD
SEAGRAVE ROAD
LANGTRY PL.
RICKETT ST.

WEST BROMPTON

FINBOROUGH ROAD
A3220
GARDENS

†

BROMPTON

CEMETERY

WEST BROMPTON

ROAD NORTH
LILLIE ROAD

Pav.
School

NORMAND PARK
lham ools
LILLIE A3218
Fitrooms

P

Brompton Park

Sch.

ROAD

Brompton Park

School

ROAD END RD.
B317

†
Sch.

Chelsea FC (Stamford Bridge)
Chelsea Village

LILLIE
A3219
DAWES
HOMESTEAD ROAD
BISHOPS RD.
Superstore
Police Sta.
A304 FULHAM
ROAD END RD.
NTH. ROAD

FULHAM BROADWAY
FULHAM BROADWAY
HARWOOD R.
FULHAM
B318

Coll.
†
Town Hall

David Lloyd Leisure
Bovril Gate

A304

27

0   100 m
Scale

Horse Guards Parade
28 July – 9 August

Getting to the Venue

You should approach Horse Guards Parade from Trafalgar Square to the north of the venue, or from St. James's Park from the south. There will be no access to the venue from Whitehall or The Mall.

≈ There are three National Rail stations within walking distance of Horse Guards Parade – London Charing Cross (600m), London Victoria (1,100m) and London Waterloo (1,900m).

⊖ The recommended stations for Horse Guards Parade are:
Charing Cross on the Bakerloo and Northern lines;
Green Park on the Jubilee, Piccadilly and Victoria lines;
Piccadilly Circus on the Piccadilly and Bakerloo lines;
Victoria on the Victoria, Circle and District lines; and
Embankment on the Bakerloo, Circle, District and Northern lines.

🚌 London has an extensive bus network and there are routes and stops in the area.

🚢 Thames river services run from Putney in the west and Woolwich Arsenal and Greenwich in the east. Embankment and Westminster Piers are the closest.

♿P Limited, pre-booked parking will be provided for disabled spectators who are UK Blue Badge holders or members of an equivalent national scheme.

🚶 It is easy to walk to Horse Guards Parade from all over central London.

🚕 There will be a taxi and private hire vehicle drop-off point close to the venue.

🚲P Free, secure, managed cycle parking will be provided at various locations around central London.

•••• Recommended spectator access routes to and from the venue.

◀🚶▶ Venue entrance or exit.

Ⓛ London 2012 Live Site, Trafalgar Square. (Paralympic Games only).

Horse Guards Parade dates from 1745, and takes its name from the soldiers who have provided protection for the monarch since 1660.

Scan for the latest transport information

Beach Volleyball

Beach Volleyball made its Olympic debut at Atlanta 1996. Since then it has become one of the most popular spectator sports at the Games.

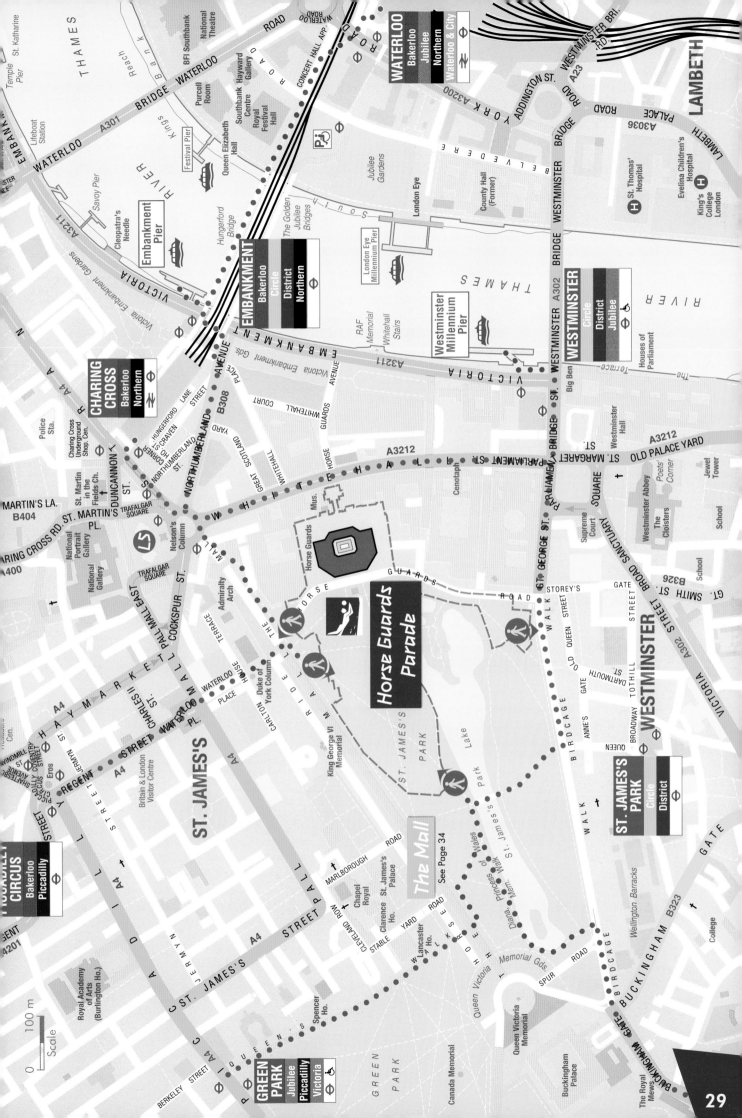

Hyde Park

The largest of London's Royal Parks, Hyde Park has been open to the public since 1637.

The park is expected to be home to the music, theatre, film and cultural events that will take place throughout the summer of 2012.

Getting to the Venue

There are two National Rail stations within walking distance of Hyde Park: London Paddington and London Victoria.

There are many London Underground stations located within five to ten minutes walking distance of Hyde Park. The recommended stations during games time are:

Hyde Park Corner (exit only 10am - 10pm), Marble Arch (exit only 10am - 10pm), Bond Street, Edgeware Road, Green Park, Knightsbridge, Victoria and Paddington.

London has an extensive bus network and there are routes and stops close to the venue.

Limited, pre-booked parking will be provided for disabled spectators who are UK Blue Badge holders or members of an equivalent national scheme.

Walking is the easiest way to reach Hyde Park from most parts of central London.

Taxis and private hire vehicles are not able to drop off inside Hyde Park. There will be a taxi and private hire vehicle drop-off point close to the venue.

Free, secure, managed cycle parking will be provided at various locations around central London.

•••• Recommended spectator access routes to and from the venue.

Venue entrance or exit.

London 2012 Live Site, Hyde Park. (Olympic Games only).

London 2012 shop.

Scan for the latest transport information

Triathlon

Triathlon races combine swimming, cycling and running, in that order. For the Olympic Games, the men's and women's Triathlons will consist of a 1500m swim, a 40km bike ride and a 10km run.

10km Marathon Swimming

At the first few modern Olympic Games, Swimming events were held in open water. At Paris in 1900, for instance, they took place in the River Seine.

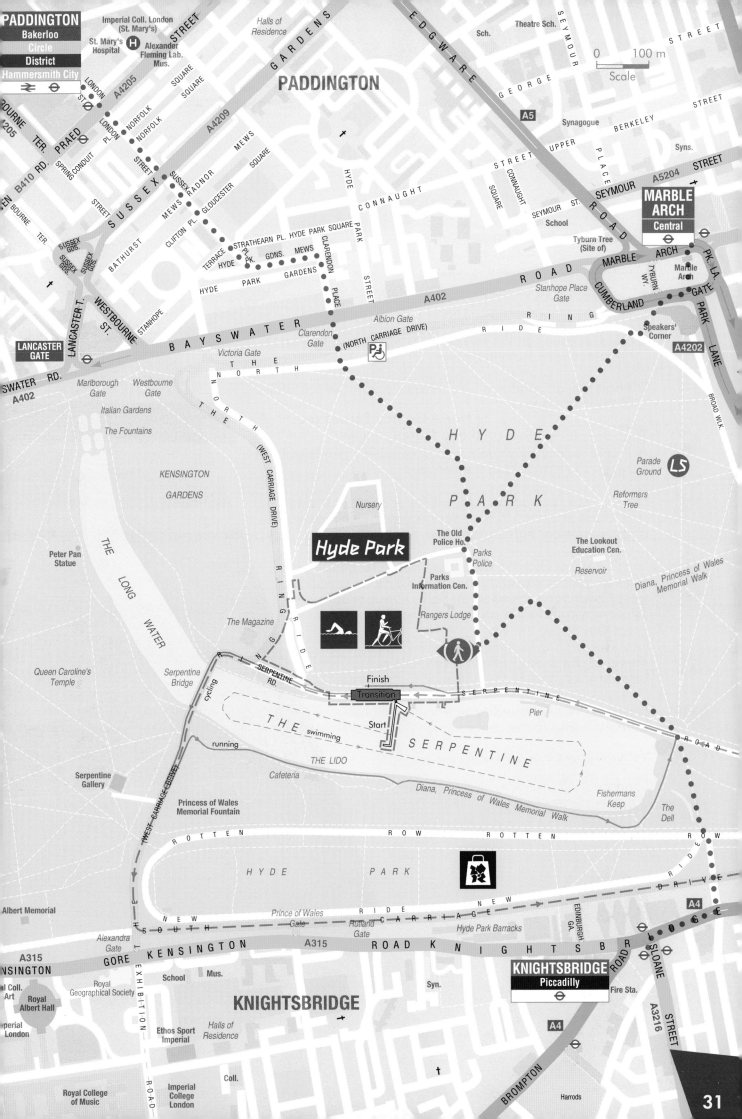

Lord's Cricket Ground
27 July – 3 August

Lord's is the home ground of Middlesex County Cricket Club, and has been a venue for top-class cricket since the late 19th century.

Getting to the Venue

Lord's Cricket Ground is located within walking distance of London Paddington station.

The recommended station for Lord's Cricket Ground is St. John's Wood on the Jubilee line, which is approximately 10 minutes walk from the venue.

London has an extensive bus network and there are routes and stops in the area.

The nearest step-free station is Kings Cross St Pancras. A shuttle service for people with accessibility needs will run between the station and the venue.

Limited, pre-booked parking will be provided for disabled spectators who are UK Blue Badge holders or members of an equivalent national scheme.

Lord's Cricket Ground is approximately 10 minutes walk from St. John's Wood station, and 40 minutes walk from Oxford Street and Hyde Park. The Jubilee Greenway runs to the south of the venue and is a great way to see the city.

There will be a drop-off point for taxis and private hire vehicles close to the entrance to the venue.

Free, secure, managed cycle parking will be provided close to the venue.

Recommended spectator access routes to and from the venue.

Venue entrance or exit.

Scan for the latest transport information

Archery

Archery dates back around 10,000 years, when bows and arrows were first used for hunting and warfare, before it developed as a competitive activity in medieval England.

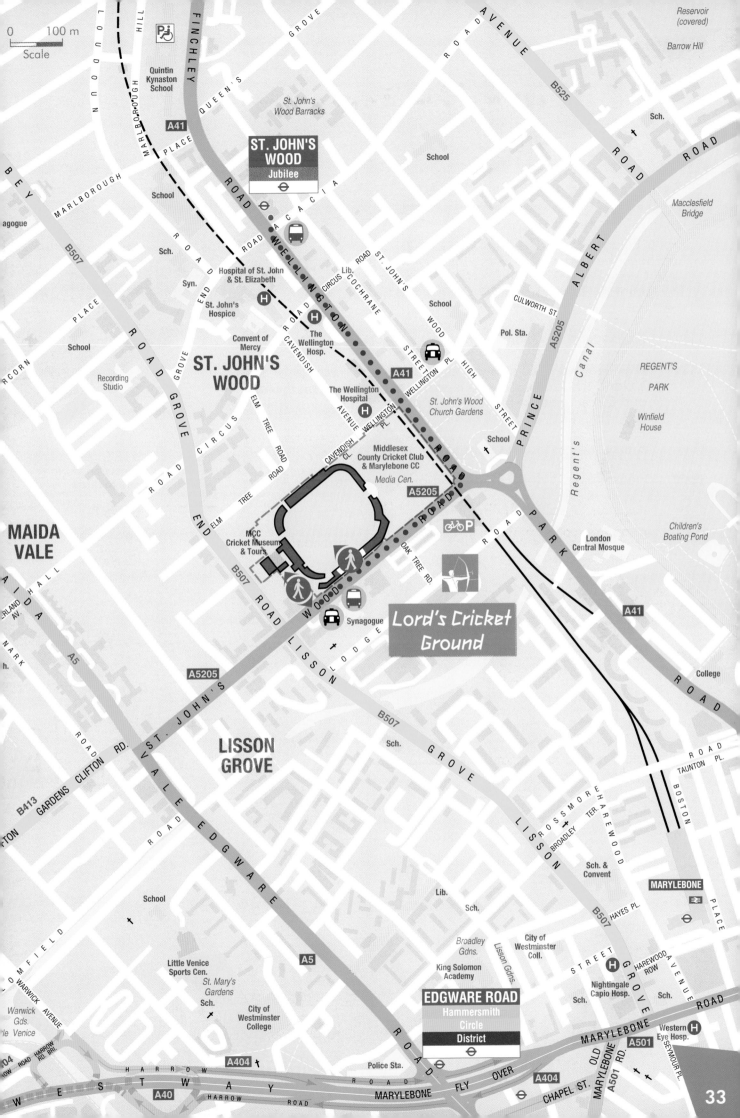

Reservoir (covered)

Barrow Hill

Quintin Kynaston School

Macclesfield Bridge

St. John's Wood Barracks

School

School

CULWORTH ST.

Pol. Sta.

REGENT'S PARK

Hospital of St. John & St. Elizabeth

St. John's Hospice

Winfield House

ST. JOHN'S WOOD

The Wellington Hosp.

Convent of Mercy

St. John's Wood Church Gardens

School

Recording Studio

The Wellington Hospital

School

Middlesex County Cricket Club & Marylebone CC

Media Cen.

MAIDA VALE

MCC Cricket Museum & Tours

Children's Boating Pond

Lord's Cricket Ground

London Central Mosque

Synagogue

LISSON GROVE

Sch.

College

Sch. & Convent

TAUNTON PL.

Lib.

Sch.

HAYES PL.

Broadley Gdns.

City of Westminster Coll.

King Solomon Academy

School

Little Venice Sports Cen.

St. Mary's Gardens

Sch.

City of Westminster College

Nightingale Capio Hosp.

Western Eye Hosp.

Warwick Gds.

Little Venice

Police Sta.

WESTWAY

HARROW ROAD

MARYLEBONE FLY OVER

MARYLEBONE

CHAPEL ST.

OLD MARYLEBONE RD.

SEYMOUR PL.

0 — 100 m
Scale

The Mall

Cycling-Road Race: 28, 29 July

Marathon: 5, 12 August

Race Walk: 4, 11 August

Marathon:
9 September

Getting to the Venue

If you are heading to watch any of the events being held on The Mall, you should approach the venue from the south (Victoria) or west (Green Park). You will not be able to access The Mall from Trafalgar Square, as this will be used for spectators attending events at Horse Guards Parade.

 Please refer to 'Getting to the Venue' for Horse Guards Parade.

 The recommended stations for The Mall are: Victoria on the Victoria, District and Circle lines; St James's Park on the District and Circle lines; and Green Park on the Jubilee, Piccadilly and Victoria lines.

 Please refer to Horse Guards Parade, on page 28.

 Please refer to Horse Guards Parade, on page 28.

 It is easy to walk to The Mall from all over central London.

 Free, secure, managed cycle parking will be provided at various locations around central London.

 Recommended spectator access routes to and from the venue.

 Venue entrance or exit.

 London 2012 Live Site, Traflagar Square. (Paralympic Games only).

The Mall

Scan for the latest transport information

Marathons
42.195km

Race Walk
50km for men and 20km for women

Cycling - Road Race
See Page 36

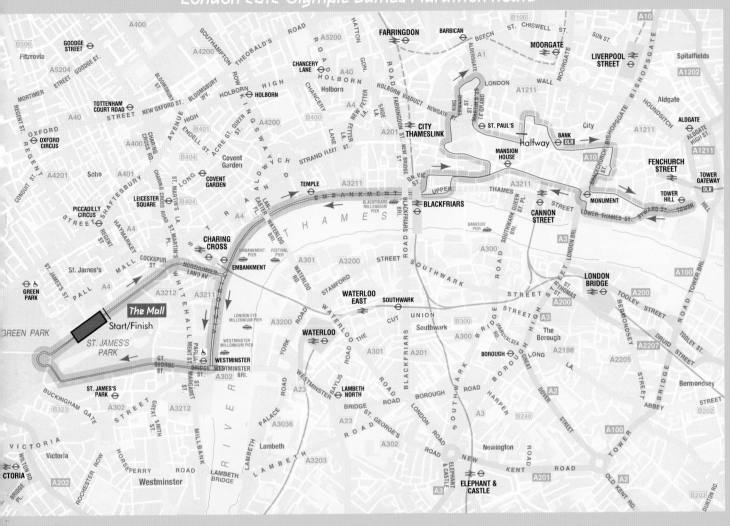

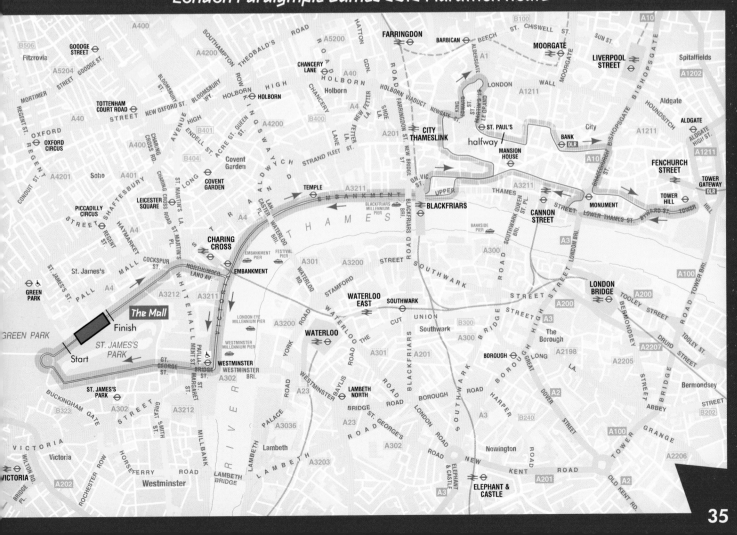

The Mall - Cycling Road Race

28 July - men's race, 29 July - women's race

The Road Race will start and finish on The Mall and cover approximately 250km for men, 140km for women.

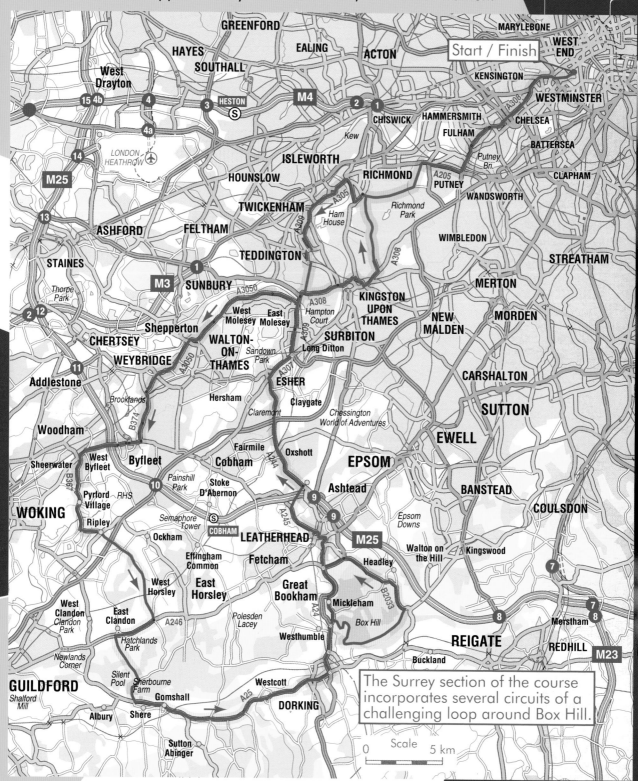

The Surrey section of the course incorporates several circuits of a challenging loop around Box Hill.

The first Olympic Games Cycling Road Race in 1896 was from Athens to Marathon, and back again.

There will be restricted access areas at The Mall in central London and Box Hill in Surrey.

Local people should plan their travel carefully using council websites to find out about any impact on travel plans.

Beijing 2008 Olympic Games
Grete Treier of Estonia competes
in the women's Road Cycling event

38

London River Zone

Scale:
0 — 500 m

39

ExCeL

28 July – 12 August

30 August – 9 September

ExCeL is situated near London City Airport

Getting to the Venue

DLR ExCeL is on the Beckton and Woolwich Arsenal DLR lines. The venue can be reached from Bank or Tower Gateway stations in central London, on the Woolwich Arsenal or Beckton lines.
Spectators should arrive at Custom House (on the Beckton line) or West Silvertown (on the Woolwich Arsenal line) and depart from Prince Regent or Pontoon Dock station.

There will be a 2012 Games coach service provided to ExCeL from a range of locations. Services will be timed to arrive at the venue for the start of sessions.

London has an extensive bus network and there are routes and stops in the area.

Limited, pre-booked parking will be provided for disabled spectators who are UK Blue Badge holders or members of an equivalent national scheme.

P+R There will be park-and-ride services provided for this venue.

ExCeL is located close to the Gallion's Reach 'greenway' route in the east, the Greenwich foot tunnel to the south and the Elevated Greenway to the north.

A drop-off and pick up-point will be provided at the western end of the venue for taxi and private hire vehicles.

ExCeL is located on recommended cycling routes from Beckton, Plaistow and Canning Town. These routes include some off-highway sections. National Cycle Network route 13 runs to the south of the venue. Free, secure, managed cycle parking will be provided at the venue.

•••• Recommended spectator access routes to and from the venue.

Venue entrance or exit.

Scan for the latest transport information

Boccia
Fencing
Judo
Powerlifting
Table Tennis
Volleyball (Sitting)

Boxing
Fencing
Judo
Table Tennis
<Taekwondo
Weightlifting
Wrestling

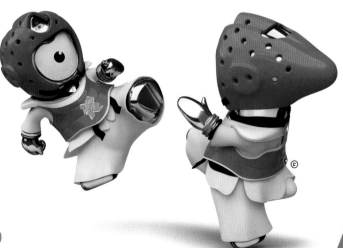

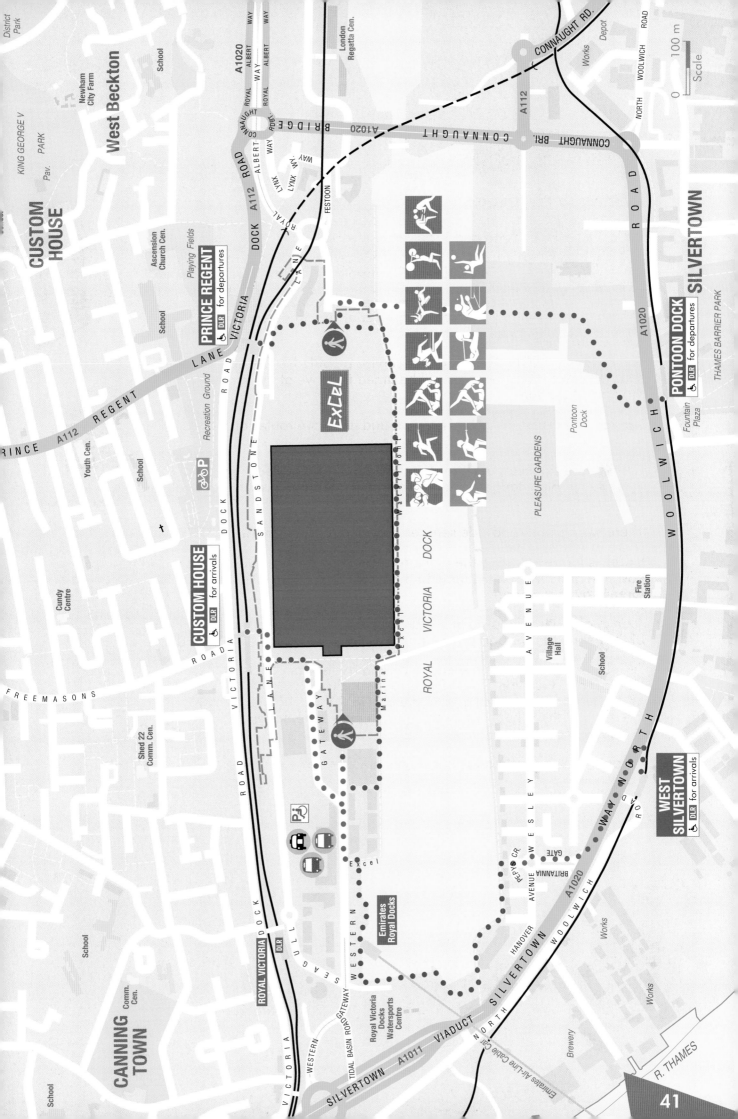

41

Greenwich Park

28 July - 12 August

Getting to the Venue

Trains to Greenwich, Blackheath and Maze Hill leave from London Charing Cross or London Cannon Street. Trains to Blackheath also leave from London Victoria.

DLR The DLR provides easy access to Greenwich Park from central London and Stratford. DLR routes to Greenwich run from Bank in central London, Stratford in the east and Lewisham in the south. Use Greenwich station, not Cutty Sark for Maritime Greenwich, which will be closed at peak periods during the Games.

London has an extensive bus network and there are routes and stops in the area.

30 July 2012

P+R The Cross Country event park-and-ride services will run to Greenwich Park on day three of the Eventing competition.

The Cross Country event coach services will run to Greenwich Park from a range of locations on day three of the Eventing competition.

Scan for the latest transport information

There are three scheduled river services departing from piers in central London to Greenwich, either direct or stopping at various piers along the way. Greenwich Pier is 500m from the venue's entrance.

Greenwich Pier and Thames river services are suitable for a range of disabled people, including wheelchair users. However, pier gradients may be affected by tides. A 'Ramp Rider', a horizontal mechanical lift, is available at Greenwich Pier for wheelchair users to use during low tides, when the pier gradient becomes steeper.

Walking is a good way to reach Greenwich Park from many locations. Greenwich is linked to the Docklands on the north of the river by the Greenwich foot tunnel and is also on the Thames Path, which runs along the River Thames.

There will be a taxi and private hire vehicle drop-off point close to the venue.

Greenwich Park is well-located for spectators wishing to cycle. It is located on a number of cycle paths that run along the River Thames and on national cycle routes 1, 4 and 21. Free, secure, managed cycle parking will be provided at the venue.

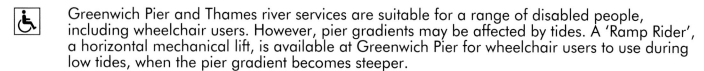

• • • • Recommended spectator access routes to and from the venue.

 Venue entrance or exit.

Equestrian
Para-Equestrian Dressage

Equestrian
Jumping, Dressage and Eventing

Modern Pentathlon
Riding event and the combined running and shooting event

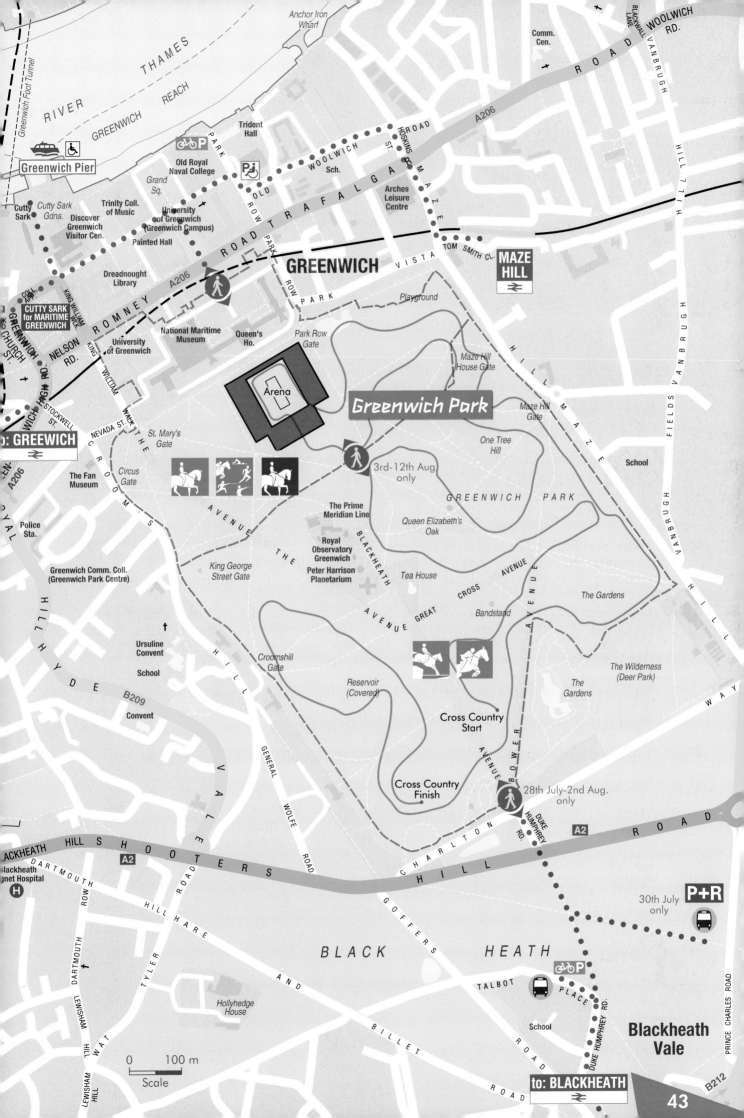

RIVER THAMES

GREENWICH REACH

Anchor Iron
Wharf

Comm.
Cen.

BLACKWALL LANE

WOOLWICH ROAD

VANBRUGH HILL

Greenwich Foot Tunnel

Greenwich Pier

Cutty Sark

Cutty Sark Gdns.

Discover Greenwich Visitor Cen.

Trinity Coll. of Music

University of Greenwich (Greenwich Campus)

Painted Hall

Old Royal Naval College

Grand Sq.

Trident Hall

A206

WOOLWICH ROAD

OLD WOOLWICH ROAD

HOSKINS ST.

Sch.

Arches Leisure Centre

TOM SMITH CL.

MAZE HILL

VANBRUGH FIELDS

School

ROAD TRAFALGAR

PARK ROW

GREENWICH

VISTA

Dreadnought Library

ROMNEY ROAD A206

KING WILLIAM WALK

NELSON RD.

CUTTY SARK for MARITIME GREENWICH

COLL. APP.

to: GREEWICH

STOCKWELL ST.

GREENWICH HIGH RD.

CHURCH ST.

National Maritime Museum

University of Greenwich

Queen's Ho.

Park Row Gate

Playground

Maze Hill House Gate

Maze Hill Gate

MAZE HILL

NEVADA ST.

CROOMS HILL

The Fan Museum

St. Mary's Gate

Circus Gate

Arena

Greenwich Park

One Tree Hill

3rd-12th Aug only

GREENWICH PARK

Police Sta.

Greenwich Comm. Coll. (Greenwich Park Centre)

THE AVENUE

King George Street Gate

The Prime Meridian Line

Royal Observatory Greenwich

Peter Harrison Planetarium

BLACKHEATH AVENUE

Queen Elizabeth's Oak

Tea House

GREAT CROSS AVENUE

Bandstand

The Gardens

The Gardens

The Wilderness (Deer Park)

HYDE VALE

B209

Ursuline Convent School

Convent

Croomshill Gate

Reservoir (Covered)

Cross Country Start

Cross Country Finish

BOWER AVENUE

28th July-2nd Aug. only

CHARLTON WAY

VANBRUGH HILL

WAY

BLACKHEATH HILL

A2

SHOOTERS HILL ROAD

DARTMOUTH ROW

HILL

TYLER ST.

HARE AND BILLET ROAD

GENERAL WOLFE ROAD

DUKE HUMPHREY RD.

A2 ROAD

30th July only

P+R

Blackheath Cynet Hospital

H

LEWISHAM HILL

DARTMOUTH HILL

LEWISHAM WAY

Hollyhedge House

BLACK HEATH

GOFFERS ROAD

Talbot PLACE

DUKE HUMPHREY RD.

School

Blackheath Vale

PRINCE CHARLES ROAD

0   100 m
Scale

to: BLACKHEATH

B212

43

North Greenwich Arena

28 July – 12 August
30 August – 8 September

Originally built for the Millennium celebrations, this venue has now been transformed into a sports and entertainment arena with shops, restaurants and more.

This venue is not near the Greenwich National Rail and DLR station. The venue's car parks will not be available during the Games.

Getting to the Venue

 North Greenwich Arena can be accessed by National Rail services to Charlton station. The station has direct services from London Charing Cross, London Cannon Street and Kent, with connections from the rest of the National Rail network.

 North Greenwich station on the Jubilee line is next to the venue.

 Shuttle buses will run from Charlton station to North Greenwich Arena at peak times.

 There will be a 2012 Games coach service drop off at West Parkside.

 London has an extensive bus network and there are routes and stops in the area.

 North Greenwich Arena is served from central London by an express river bus service and a more leisurely river tours service, both stopping at North Greenwich Pier.

 North Greenwich Arena is on the Thames Path National Trail from Greenwich, which links to the south-east London Green Chain at the Thames Barrier. Section 6 of the Jubilee Greenway runs past the venue.

 There will be a taxi and private hire vehicle drop-off point close to the venue.

 The venue is located on the 'greenway' cycle route from Greenwich. There are a number of cycle routes that run along the River Thames in this part of London. Free, secure, managed cycle parking will be provided at the venue.

• • • • Recommended spectator access routes to and from the venue.

 Venue entrance or exit.

Scan for the latest transport information

Wheelchair Basketball featured at the first Paralympic Games in Rome 1960

Wheelchair Basketball

Gymnastics- Trampoline
springing to heights of up to 10m

Basketball
men's and women's finals

Artistic
perfect symmetry

44

EAST INDIA DOCK ROAD

A13

SOUTH BROMLEY

A1261

EAST INDIA
DLR

Blackwall

BLACKWALL

ASPEN

ASPEN WAY

LEAMOUTH RD.

Works

Orchard Wharf

Silvocea Wharf

Bridge Wharf

Crown Wharf

Bow Creek Ecology Park

BOW

LOWER

ORCHARD PLACE

ORCHARD PLACE

Jubilee Wharf

BOW CREEK

CREEK

LEAMOUTH

LEA

RIVER LEA

A1020

CROSSING

SILVERTOWN A1011

VIADUCT

EAST INDIA DOCK BASIN

Virginia Quay Pk.

Nature Reserve

Trinity Pier

Works

Virginia Quay

Pier

Blackwall Pier

Thames Wharf

Graving Dock

Offices

Blackwall Stairs

Northumberland Wharf

BLACKWALL

A102

TUNNEL

A102

TUNNEL

JUBILEE

GREENWAY

Ordnance Wharf

RIVER

REACH

THAMES

PATH

Blackwall Point

North Greenwich Pier ♿

London City Airport Pier

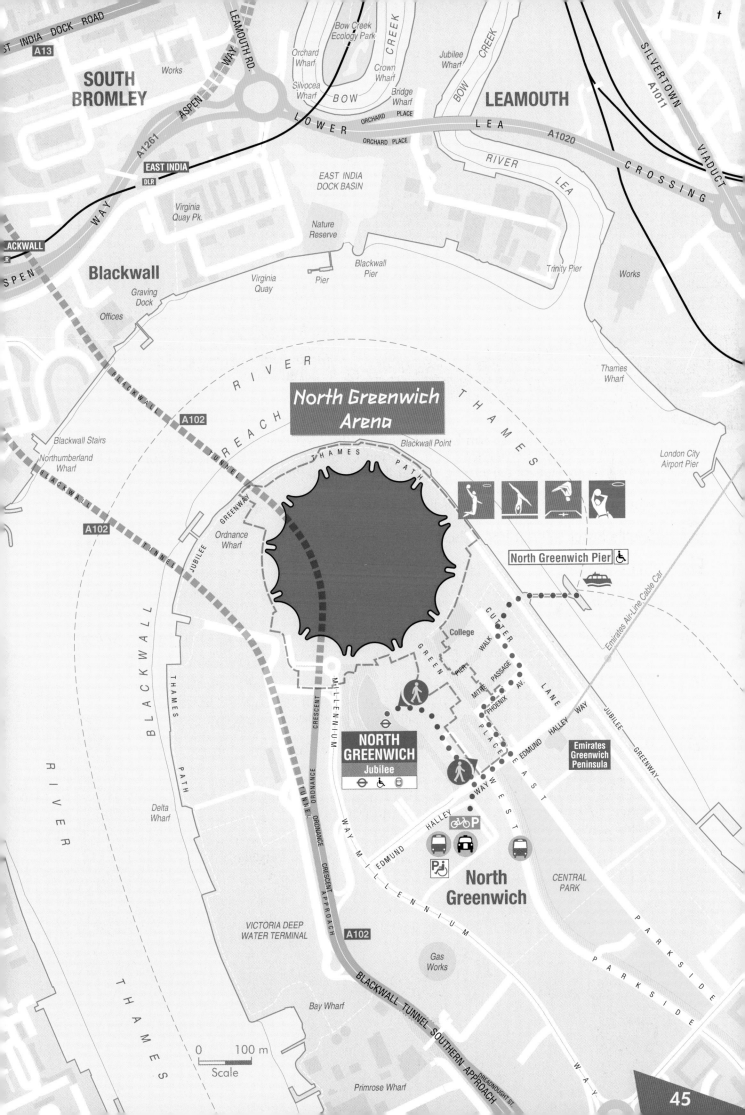

North Greenwich Arena

Emirates Air-Line Cable Car

College

CUTTER

GREEN

PIER

WALK

MITRE

PASSAGE

PHOENIX AV.

PLACE

EDMUND HALLEY WAY

LANE

JUBILEE GREENWAY

BLACKWALL

THAMES

PATH

RIVER

THAMES

Delta Wharf

CRESCENT

MILLENNIUM

ORDNANCE

TUNNEL

CRESCENT APPROACH

A102

NORTH GREENWICH
Jubilee
🚇 ♿ 🚆

HALLEY

WAY

WEST

EAST

WAY

🚲 P

🚌 🚕 🚌

P♿

Emirates Greenwich Peninsula

North Greenwich

CENTRAL PARK

PARKSIDE

PARKSIDE

EDMUND HALLEY

WAY MILLENNIUM

WAY

VICTORIA DEEP WATER TERMINAL

Gas Works

BLACKWALL TUNNEL SOUTHERN APPROACH

DREADNOUGHT ST.

Bay Wharf

Primrose Wharf

0   100 m
Scale

45

The Royal Artillery Barracks

28 July – 6 August

30 August – 6 September

The London port of Woolwich has a long military history and the construction of the current Royal Artillery Barracks buildings began in 1776.

Getting to the Venue

 Woolwich Arsenal station is a 20-minute walk or a shuttle-bus journey from the venue. The station has direct services from London Charing Cross, London Cannon Street and Kent, with connections from the rest of the National Rail network.

 An accessible shuttle will be provided from Woolwich Arsenal station to and from the venue for spectators with accessibility needs.

 There will be a 2012 Games coach service drop off near the venue.

DLR The DLR to Woolwich Arsenal leaves from Bank station in central London. The DLR also links Stratford with the venue.

 London has an extensive bus network and there are many routes and stops in the area.

 Woolwich is on the south bank of the River Thames and can be accessed by a river service operating from North Greenwich Pier to Woolwich Arsenal Pier.

 The Royal Artillery Barracks are a 20 minute uphill walk from Woolwich Arsenal station and a 25-minute walk from Woolwich Arsenal Pier. Sections 4 and 5 of the Green Chain Walk run to the south of the venue. Section 6 of the Jubilee Greenway runs along the northern edge of the venue.

Scan for the latest transport information

 There will be a taxi and private hire vehicle drop-off point close to the venue.

 The venue can be reached by cycle on the 'greenway' cycle route along the River Thames from Greenwich. It is also located on the National Cycle Network route 1 and the London Cycle Network route 75. Free, secure, managed cycle parking will be provided at the venue.

• • • • Recommended spectator access routes to and from the venue.

 Venue entrance or exit.

LS London 2012 Live Site, General Gordon Place, Woolwich.

Shooting

Nearly 400 competitors will be shooting for gold across 15 dramatic events.

Archery

featured at the first Stoke Mandeville Games in 1948, the direct precursor to the Paralympic Games.

Shooting

Paralympic Shooting legend Isabel Newstead was one of Britain's greatest-ever Paralympians.

46

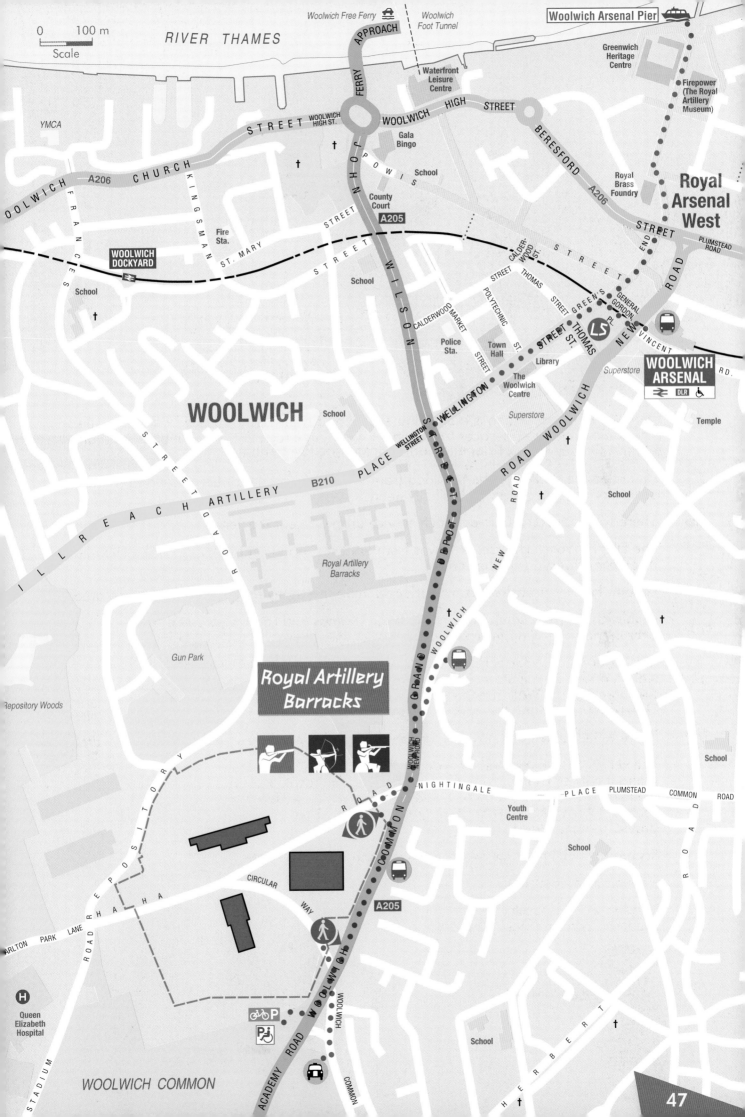

Scale

0   100 m

RIVER THAMES

Woolwich Free Ferry
Woolwich Foot Tunnel

Woolwich Arsenal Pier

Greenwich Heritage Centre

Firepower
(The Royal Artillery Museum)

Royal Arsenal West

FERRY APPROACH

WOOLWICH HIGH ST.

WOOLWICH HIGH STREET

YMCA

CHURCH STREET
A206

WOOLWICH DOCKYARD

School

Fire Sta.

KINGSMAN STREET

FRANCES

ST. MARY STREET

Waterfront Leisure Centre

Gala Bingo

School

County Court

A205

JOHN WILSON STREET

POWIS STREET

BERESFORD STREET A206

Royal Brass Foundry

END

STREET

PLUMSTEAD ROAD

CALDERWOOD ST.

STREET THOMAS STREET

POLYTECHNIC ST.

GREEN'S PL.

GENERAL GORDON

NEW ROAD

NEW VINCENT RD.

WOOLWICH ARSENAL

LS

Superstore

School

CALDERWOOD MARKET

Police Sta.

Town Hall

Library

The Woolwich Centre

WELLINGTON STREET

THOMAS STREET

Superstore

WOOLWICH

School

WOOLWICH ROAD

Temple

School

ILL REACH

ARTILLERY PLACE B210

REPOSITORY ROAD

Gun Park

Repository Woods

Royal Artillery Barracks

Royal Artillery Barracks

GRAND DEPOT ROAD

WOOLWICH NEW ROAD

WOOLWICH

School

NEW ROAD

Youth Centre

NIGHTINGALE PLACE

PLUMSTEAD COMMON ROAD

School

HERBERT ROAD

CIRCULAR WAY

COMMON

A205

WOOLWICH COMMON

STADIUM

CHARLTON PARK LANE

REPOSITORY ROAD

HA HA

WOOLWICH

H
Queen Elizabeth Hospital

School

WOOLWICH COMMON

47

Beijing 2008 Olympic Games
David Florence of Great Britain competes
in the Canoe Single (C1) Men's semi final.

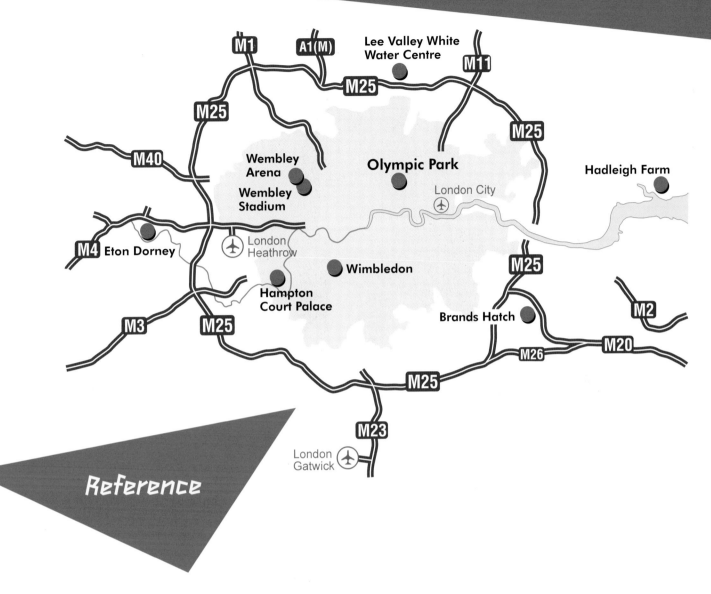

Reference

Motorway	M25	Underground	⊖	Spectator route	••••
Primary route	A12	DLR	DLR	Entrance and exit	👁
A road	A118 A118	Tram Metrolink / Tramlink	🚋	Live Site	LS
B road	B112 B112	Metro (Newcastle)	M	Venue perimeter	⌐¬
One way	→	Subway (Glasgow)	S	Visitor highlights	★
Airport	✈	Riverboat Recommended Stop	🚢 WESTMINSTER	Venue name	The Mall
Rail	Stations ⇄ Tunnel	Bus	🚌	Venue building	⬛
Tram	Stations ⇄ Tunnel	Coach	🚌		
Station names	VICTORIA	Shuttle bus	🚌	Olympic sport	🏃
Recommended stations	WEMBLEY	Taxi	🚕	Paralympic sport	♿
Step-free station	♿	Cycle parking	🚲P	Built up area	
National rail	⇌	Park and ride Pick up / Drop off	P+R		
Overground	⊖	Blue Badge parking	♿P	Parks and rivers	

Brands Hatch - Kent
5 - 8 September

Travelling to Brands Hatch

Brands Hatch is situated on the A20 near West Kingsdown. Just 5 kms from junction 3 (Swanley) of the M25 motorway.

 London Gatwick Airport is the UK's second largest airport and the busiest single-runway airport in the world. The airport is 45 kms south of London with excellent public transport links.

 Ebbsfleet International in Gravesham, Kent is located off junction 2 (A2) from the M25 London orbital motorway. Ebbsfleet International station provides direct train services to Europe and Central London.

Sevenoaks station is the recommended station, 10km from the venue. It can be reached by National Rail from London Victoria and London Blackfriars stations in central London.

 Accessibility

London Gatwick Airport has facilities for passengers with reduced mobility.
Tel:+44 (0)844 892 0322 and select option 2.

Visitor Highlights
☆

www.visitkent.co.uk

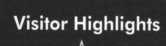

Lullingstone Roman Villa

Among the most outstanding Roman villa survivals in Britain, Lullingstone provides a unique all weather family day out.

Ightham Mote

Built nearly 700 years ago, this romantic moated manor house has been owned by medieval knights courtiers to Henry VIII and high-society Victorians.

Knole

Knole has been shown off to visitors for the past 500 years. Thirteen show rooms remain much as they were in the 18th century. Knole is set at the heart of the only remaining medieval deer park in Kent.

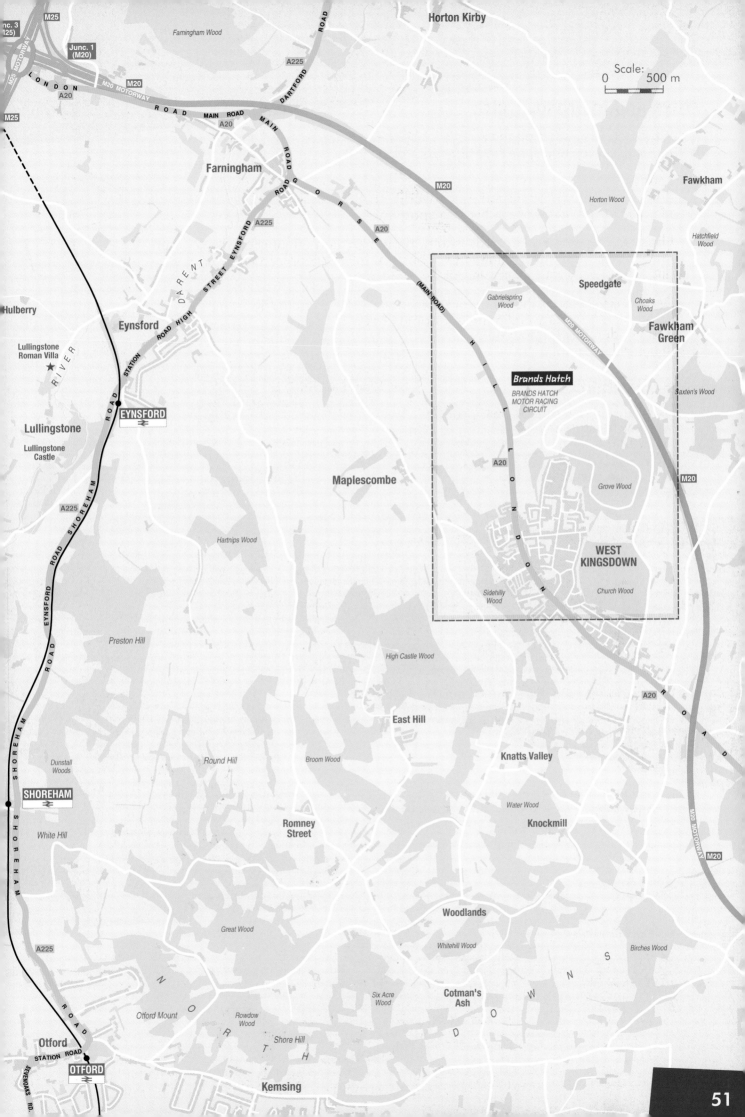

Horton Kirby

Farningham Wood

M25
Junc. 3
(125)

Junc. 1
(M20)

M20

M25

M20 MOTORWAY

LONDON
A20

A225

DARTFORD

MAIN ROAD

A20

M20

ROAD

MAIN ROAD

MAIN ROAD

Farningham

GORSE

Fawkham

A20

Horton Wood

Hatchfield
Wood

A225

STREET EYNSFORD

M25

DARENT

ROAD HIGH

ROAD STATION

Eynsford

Hulberry

Lullingstone
Roman Villa

RIVER

EYNSFORD

Lullingstone

Lullingstone
Castle

A225

EYNSFORD ROAD SHOREHAM

SHOREHAM ROAD

Speedgate

Gabrielspring
Wood

Choaks
Wood

Fawkham
Green

HILL

Saxten's Wood

Brands Hatch

BRANDS HATCH
MOTOR RACING
CIRCUIT

A20

(MAIN ROAD)

LONDON

M20

M20 MOTORWAY

Maplescombe

Grove Wood

WEST
KINGSDOWN

Hartnips Wood

Preston Hill

Sidehilly
Wood

Church Wood

High Castle Wood

A20

ROAD

East Hill

Knatts Valley

Dunstall
Woods

Round Hill

Broom Wood

SHOREHAM

White Hill

Romney
Street

Water Wood

Knockmill

M20 MOTORWAY

M20

Great Wood

Woodlands

Whitehill Wood

Birches Wood

A225

N

O

R

T

H

Otford Mount

Rowdow
Wood

Six Acre
Wood

Cotman's
Ash

D

O

W

N

S

Shore Hill

Otford

STATION ROAD

SEVENOAKS RD.

OTFORD

Kemsing

Scale:
0   500 m

51

Brands Hatch
5 - 8 September

Getting to the Venue

🚌 Travel from central London to Sevenoaks station is included with the event ticket. Shuttle buses will run from Sevenoaks station to the venue.

🚲P There is good cycle access on a number of dedicated routes in the area. Free, secure, managed cycle parking will be provided at the venue.

🚕 There will be a taxi and private hire vehicle drop-off point close to the venue.

♿P Limited, pre-booked parking will be provided for disabled spectators who are UK Blue Badge holders or members of an equivalent national scheme.

🚶 Venue entrance or exit.

Scan for the latest transport information

It has hosted 12 runnings of the British Grand Prix between 1964 and 1986 and currently holds many British and international racing events.

Brands Hatch is an internationally-renowned motor racing circuit near Sevenoaks in Kent.

Road Cycling

Introduced as a Paralympic sport in 1984. Athletes will race in a series of events that should draw massive crowds.

Handcycling – for athletes with lower limb disabilities – was introduced at the Athens 2004 Games.

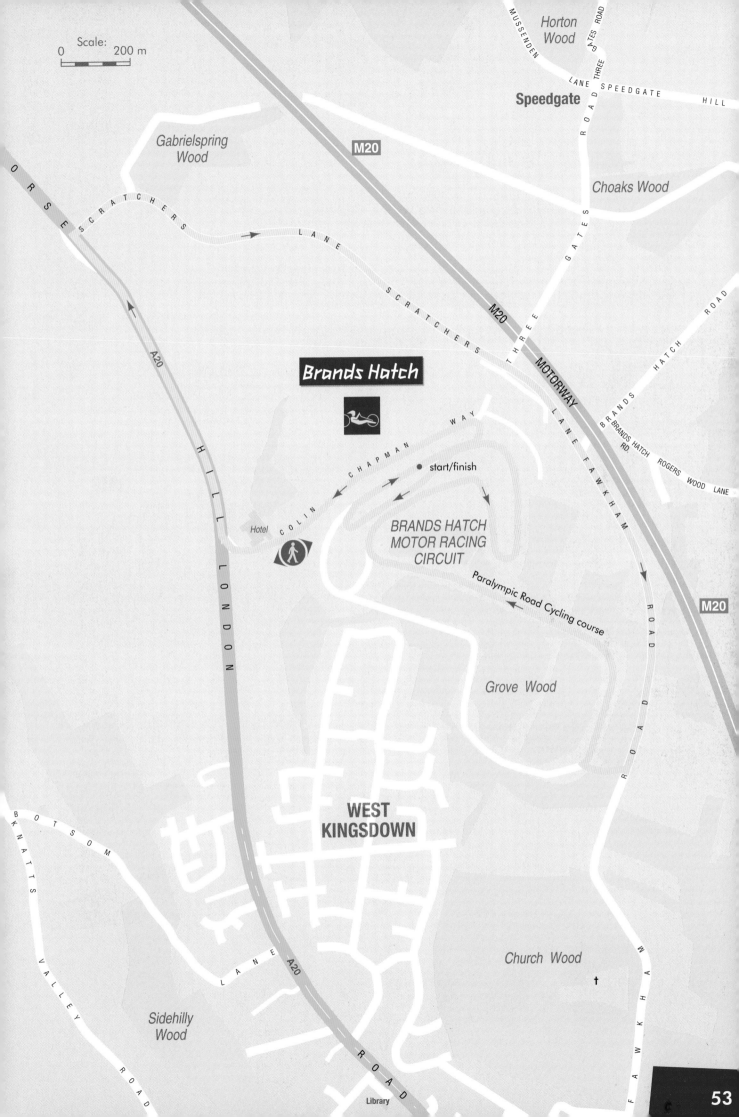

Scale:

0   200 m

Gabrielspring
Wood

Horton
Wood

Speedgate

Choaks Wood

M20

M20
MOTORWAY

Brands Hatch

SCRATCHERS LANE

SCRATCHERS

THREE GATES ROAD

MUSSENDEN LANE

SPEEDGATE HILL

B ROADS HATCH RD.

BRANDS HATCH ROAD

WOOD LANE

ROGERS

ORSE

A20

HILL LONDON

CHAPMAN WAY

COLIN

start/finish

BRANDS HATCH
MOTOR RACING
CIRCUIT

Hotel

Paralympic Road Cycling course

ROAD

THREE LANE FAWKHAM

Grove Wood

BOTSOM

KNATTS VALLEY ROAD

LANE

A20 ROAD

**WEST
KINGSDOWN**

Church Wood

FAWKHAM

Sidehilly
Wood

Library

53

Eton Dorney, Bucks.
28 July - 11 August

31 August - 2 September

Travelling to Eton Dorney

Eton Dorney is 40km outside of London and not on the London Underground network. The venue can be reached by National Rail from central London.

 Heathrow airport is 17km from Eton Dorney and has superb London connections. The Heathrow Express is a 15 minute non-stop link to London Paddington, and the London Underground Piccadilly Line runs from all terminals.

 During the Olympic Games, there are three stations providing access to Eton Dorney:

- Slough station, with direct services from Paddington, Reading and Oxford;
- Windsor & Eton Riverside station, with direct services from London Waterloo;
- Maidenhead station, with direct services from Reading.

During the Paralympic Games, Maidenhead station will not be a recommended venue station.

Accessibility

Heathrow Airport has facilities for passengers with reduced mobility. Telephone +44 (0)844 335 1801.

Slough, Maidenhead and Windsor & Eton Riverside National Rail stations are all step-free with staff assistance available.

www.windsor.gov.uk

Visitor Highlights

★ Windsor Castle

Windsor Castle is one of the largest and oldest inhabited castles in the world.

A Royal home and fortress for over 900 years, the Castle remains a working palace today.

Theme Parks

Legoland - Windsor
LEGOLAND Windsor Resort is a theme park dedicated to children aged 3-12 years old.

Thorpe Park - Chertsey
THORPE PARK has some of Europe's most extreme rides along with many attractions for younger families.

31 August – 2 September

Getting to the Venue

🚌 Shuttle buses will run from the recommended stations to the venue's transport mall.
During the Olympic Games, the mall will be located at Windsor Racecourse, a short walk from the venue across a temporary bridge over the River Thames.
During the Paralympic Games, the transport mall will be located in Big Meadows Field, to the north of the venue.

P+R Park-and-ride shuttles will be provided to the venue. They will all terminate at the venue's transport mall.

🚆 Local bus routes and stops provide access to this venue.

🚤 During the Olympic Games, a river shuttle will operate a limited service between Windsor Promenade and Windsor Racecourse, providing a fast and convenient way to travel from Windsor.

🚶 Eton Dorney is located on the north bank of the River Thames. The Thames Path north of the river runs past the venue. There is a walking route from Windsor to the transport mall at the Racecourse.

🚲P National Cycle Route Network 4 runs alongside the north perimeter of the venue. There is good cycle access on a number of dedicated routes in the area. Free, secure, managed cycle parking will be provided at the venue.

🚕 A taxi pick-up/drop-off area will be provided in the venue's transport mall.

♿P Limited, pre-booked parking will be provided in the transport mall for disabled spectators who are UK Blue Badge holders or members of an equivalent national scheme.

• • • • Recommended spectator access routes to and from the venue.

◀👤▶ Venue entrance or exit.

Scan for the latest transport information

Rowing

The newest arrival on the Paralympic programme, Rowing appeared at the Games for the first time at Beijing in 2008.

Rowing

Rowing is the only sport where competitors cross the finish line backwards.

Canoe Sprint

The Canoe Sprint 200m race will make its Olympic debut at London 2012.

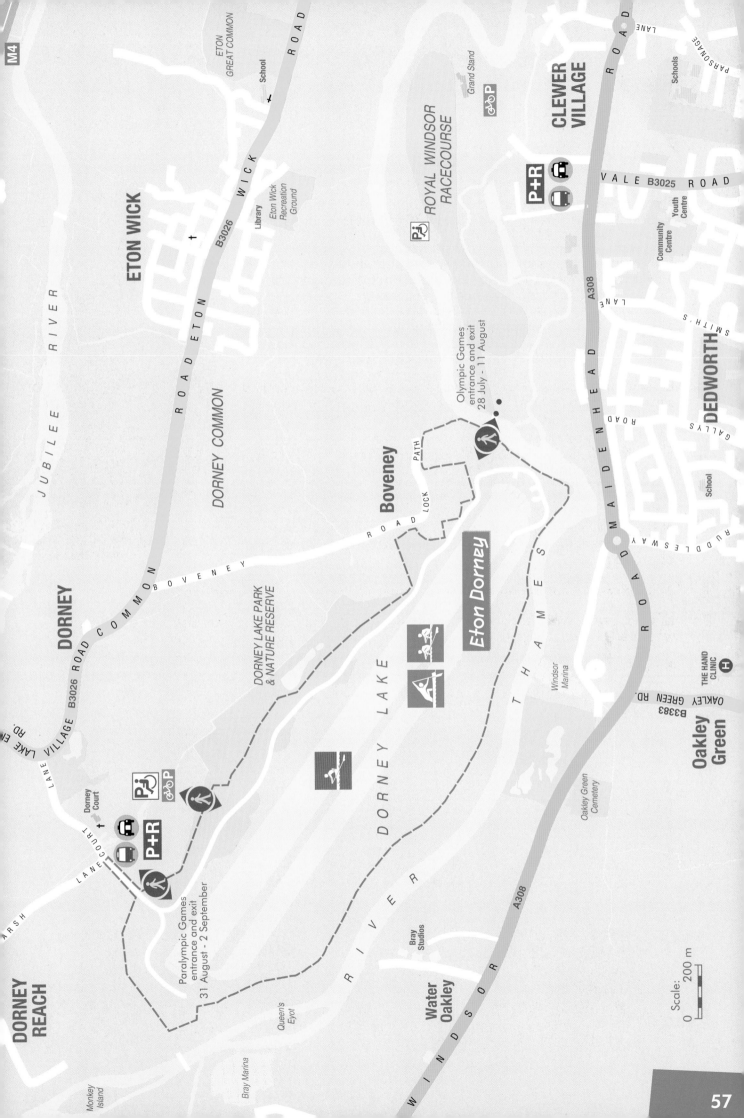

M4

ETON GREAT COMMON

School

ROAD

ETON WICK

Library

B3026

Eton Wick
Recreation
Ground

ROYAL WINDSOR
RACECOURSE

Grand Stand

P

CLEWER
VILLAGE

P+R

VALE B3025 ROAD

Community
Centre

Youth
Centre

Schools

PARSONAGE

LANE

ROAD

JUBILEE RIVER

ROAD ETON WICK

DORNEY COMMON

Boveney

PATH

LOCK

ROAD

Olympic Games
entrance and exit
28 July - 11 August

DEDWORTH

A308

MAIDENHEAD LANE

GALLYS

School

DORNEY

B3026 ROAD COMMON

BOVENEY ROAD

DORNEY LAKE PARK
& NATURE RESERVE

Eton Dorney

DORNEY LAKE

THAMES

Windsor Marina

RUDDLESWAY

MAIDENHEAD ROAD

ROAD

Oakley
Green

LANE VILLAGE

LAKE END RD.

Dorney Court

P

P+R

Paralympic Games
entrance and exit
31 August - 2 September

COURT LANE

MARSH LANE

DORNEY
REACH

WINDSOR RIVER

Bray Studios

Queen's Eyot

Oakley Green
Cemetery

B3383 OAKLEY GREEN RD.

THE HAND
CLINIC

H

Water
Oakley

A308

Bray Marina

Monkey
Island

Scale:
0   200 m

57

Travelling to Hadleigh Farm

London Southend Airport is a long-established regional airport for South East Essex and is the Eastern Gateway to London. Tel: +44 (0) 1702 608100.

A new airport railway station provides fast and frequent train services direct to Stratford (for Docklands and Canary Wharf) and to central London's Liverpool Street Station.

The recommended National Rail station for Hadleigh Farm is Leigh-on-Sea, which is a 30-minute walk or shuttle-bus journey to the venue entrance. The station has direct services from London and Southend, with connections from the rest of the National Rail network. Leigh-on-Sea station is approximately 45 minutes from London Fenchurch Street station.

Fenchurch Street station is not on the London Underground network. However, it is close to Aldgate and Tower Hill stations on the Circle line and Tower Gateway Docklands Light Railway station.

Accessibility

London Southend Airport - passengers with reduced mobility that require assistance from the car park at Southend Airport, should contact Southend Handling on +44 (0) 1702 608150 in advance of their flight.

Leigh-on-Sea station is step-free with assistance available. Accessible shuttles will run from Leigh-on-Sea station to the transport mall opposite the venue entrance.

www.visitessex.com

Audley End House and Gardens
Step back in time and watch Victorian life come to life before your eyes.

Colchester Castle Museum
The largest Norman Keep in Europe.

Visitor Highlights

Colchester Zoo
With over 270 species to see, set in 60 acres of beautiful parkland and lakes, the Zoo is well worth a visit.

ARTERIAL ROAD
A127

Pound Wood

Daws Heath

West Wood

A129

HIGH ROAD

Thundersley

Coombe Wood

ROAD KILN

A13

Tarpots

A13 LONDON ROAD HIGH WAY

A130

Belfairs Park

Great Wood

Prittle Brook

LEIGH-ON-SEA

A13 ROAD

LONDON

ROAD

B1014

LONDON

HADLEIGH

LONDON RD. HIGH STREET

ROAD

Hadleigh Farm

Sandpit Hill

Adders Hill

Plumtree Hill

Hadleigh Castle (remains of)

Shipwrights Wood

Wall Wood

Round Hill

Benfleet Downs

HADLEIGH COUNTRY PARK

BENFLEET WAY

B1006

SOUTH BENFLEET

Hope's Green

HIGH ROAD

ROAD

ST. ESSEX

HIGH

BENFLEET

FERRY ROAD

B1014

B1006

LONDON HIGH WAY

A130

A130

CANVEY WAY

A130

Belton Hills

LEIGH-ON-SEA

Leigh Marsh

Marsh End Sand

RIVER

RIVER THAMES

Two Tree Island

Hadleigh Marsh

Hadleigh Ray

Benfleet Creek

Tewkes Creek

Sunken Marsh

AVENUE CENTRAL WALL RD.

B1014

B1014

CANVEY ROAD

SOMNES AVENUE

CANVEY ISLAND

Winter Gardens

Dutch Village

East Haven Creek

Scale: 0   500 m

59

Hadleigh Farm – 11 and 12 August

Getting to the Venue

🚌 Shuttle buses will run from the recommended station Leigh-on-Sea, to the venue's entrance.

P+R Park-and-ride services will operate for this venue during the Olympic Games. Accessible parking spaces will be available at all parking sites with shuttles to the venue which are suitable for a wide range of disabled spectators including wheelchair users.

🚆 There are local bus routes and stops which provide access to this venue.

🚶 Hadleigh Farm is a 30-minute uphill walk from Leigh-on-Sea station, mostly off-road on farm tracks. Sturdy footwear is recommended.

🚲P Free, secure, managed cycle parking will be provided to the north and south of Hadleigh Farm. Park-and-cycle facilities will be provided approximately four kilometres from the venue. There are a number of off-road cycle routes to the south of the venue that provide access from the east and west.

🚕 Taxis will drop-off at Hadleigh High Street, about 10 minutes walk from the venue's entrance.

♿P Limited, pre-booked parking will be provided close to the venue for disabled spectators who are UK Blue Badge holders or members of an equivalent national scheme.

• • • • Recommended spectator access routes to and from the venue.

◀(🚶)▶ Venue entrance or exit.

Scan for the latest transport information

Mountain Bike

Having won gold in 2004 and 2008, Julien Absalon will be going for a hat-trick at London 2012.

50 men and 30 women will compete in the London 2012 Olympic Games Mountain Bike competition.

HADLEIGH

School
School

LONDON A13 ROAD

ROAD

ROAD

ROAD

CASTLE ROAD

STREET

HIGH

Library

HOMESTEAD RD.

BEECH

LANDWAY LANE

P+R

TER.

AVENUE

SEAVIEW

CASTLE

ROAD

CHAPEL

FITZWILLIAM

Hadleigh Castle
(remains of)

CASTLE

to: LEIGH-ON-SEA

Scale:

0   100 m

Hadleigh Farm

start/finish

mtb course

Cycle route from Benfleet Station

To Benfleet Station

BENFLEET

B1014 ROAD

LA

HADLEIGH
COUNTRY PARK

Hampton Court Palace is one of London's royal palaces and has housed some of Britain's most famous kings and queens, the most well known being Henry VIII.

Travelling to Hampton Court Palace

 Heathrow airport is 20km from Hampton Court Palace and has superb London connections. The Heathrow Express is a 15 minute non-stop link to London Paddington, and the London Underground Piccadilly Line runs from all Terminals.

 Hampton Court station is a 200m walk across the bridge from the venue. It has direct services from London Waterloo and Clapham Junction stations, passing through Wimbledon station, where the London Underground District Line begins.

Accessibility

Heathrow Airport has facilities for passengers with reduced mobility. Telephone +44 (0)844 335 1801.

Hampton Court station is step-free with assistance available.

Visitors with sight or mobility concerns should be aware that cyclists often ride their bicycles on the pavement of the bridge.

Scan for Hampton Court Palace

Brooklands

Opened in 1907, Brooklands was the world's first purpose-built motorsport venue, as well as one of Britain's first airfields.

Visitor Highlights

Ham House

A 400-year-old treasure trove waiting to be discovered, one of a series of grand houses and palaces alongside the River Thames.

Richmond Park

The largest Royal Park in London which is home to around 650 free roaming deer.

Theme Parks

Chessington World of Adventures
The resort includes a zoo, aquarium and a 5 star hotel.

Thorpe Park - Chertsey
Thorpe Park has some of Europe's most extreme rides.

 62

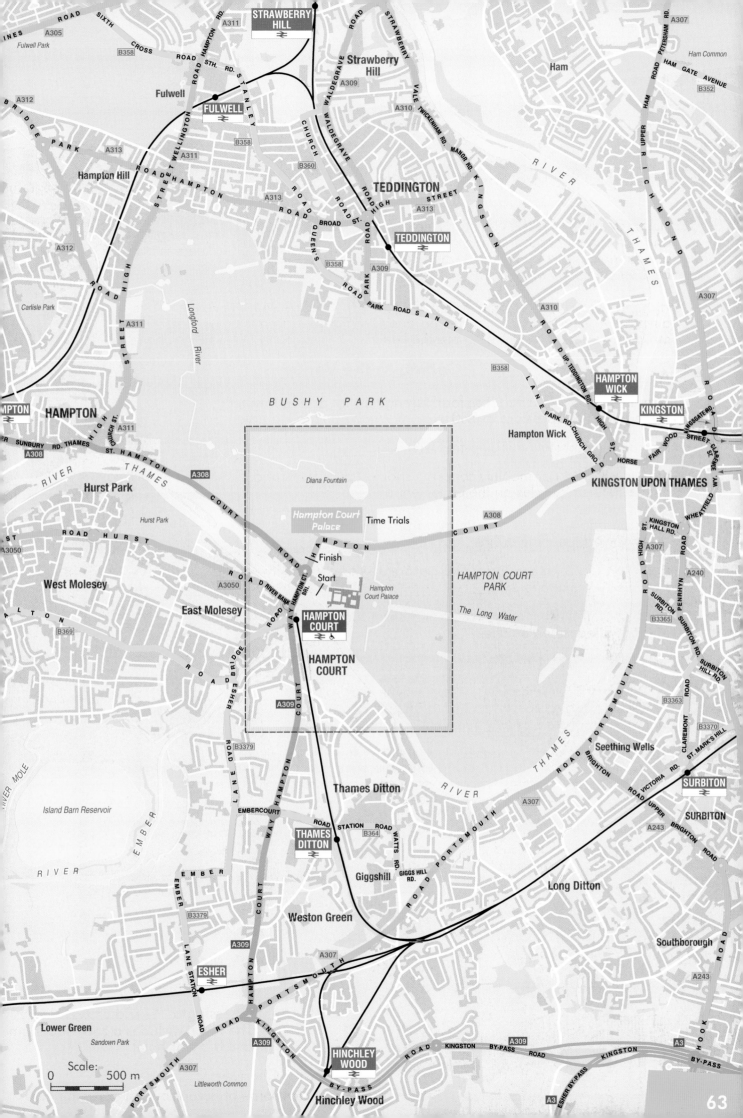

63

Hampton Court Palace
1 August

Hampton Court has a rich sporting history: The palace is home to the oldest surviving real tennis court in England, one of fewer than fifty real tennis courts in the world. There is also an 18-hole golf course in the palace grounds.

Getting to the Venue

- Wimbledon London Underground Station is 11km from the venue. National Rail services are available from Wimbledon to Hampton Court station.

- There are local bus routes and stops which provide access to this venue.

- Riverboats run from Westminster, Richmond-upon-Thames and Kingston-upon-Thames. The journey from Westminster can take up to 4 hours, depending on the tides.

- Hampton Court Palace is a 200m walk across the bridge from Hampton Court station.

- The National Cycle Network route number 4 runs along Barge Walk past the palace.

- Taxis will be available from Hampton Court Station.

- Limited, pre-booked parking will be provided close to the venue for disabled spectators who are UK Blue Badge holders or members of an equivalent national scheme.

- • • • • Recommended spectator access routes to and from the venue.

- Venue entrance or exit.

Scan for the latest transport information

Cycling - Road

Time Trial featured as a track event on the Cycling programme at the first modern Olympic Games in Athens, Greece in 1896.

The Time Trial distances are 44km for men and 29km for women. The riders start 90 seconds apart, and the winner is the rider with the fastest time over the course.

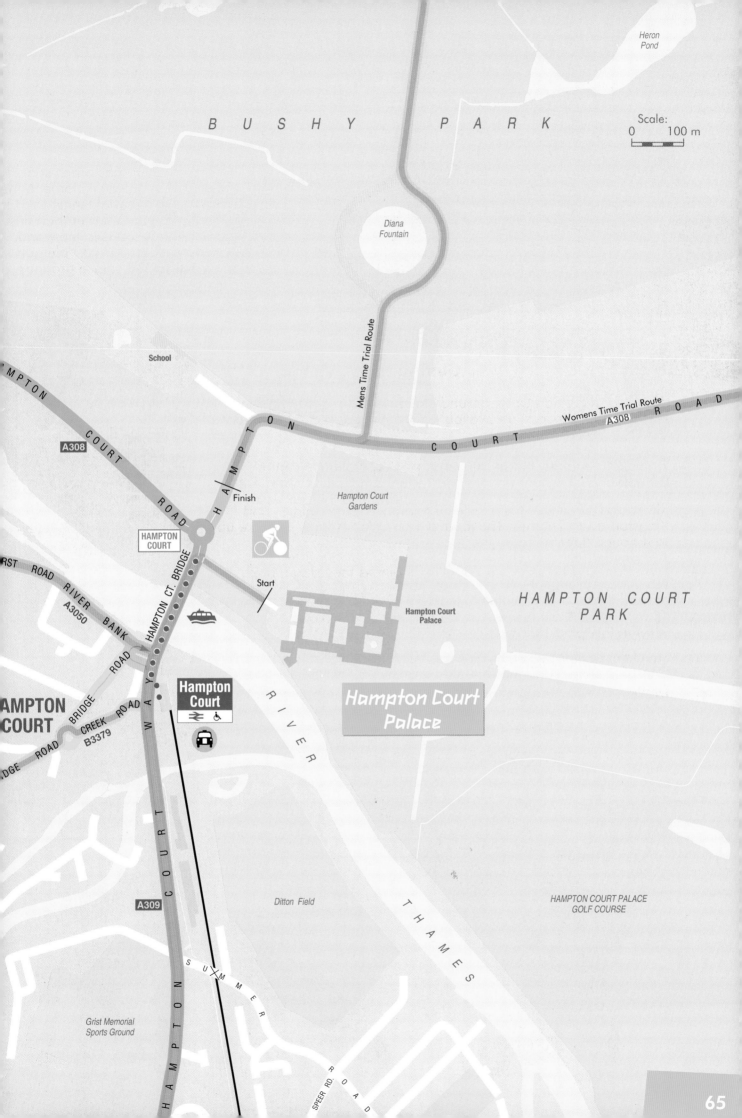

BUSHY PARK

Heron Pond

Scale:
0   100 m

Diana Fountain

Mens Time Trial Route

School

HAMPTON COURT ROAD
A308

Womens Time Trial Route
A308

HAMPTON COURT ROAD

Hampton Court Gardens

Finish

HAMPTON COURT

HAMPTON CT. BRIDGE

HURST ROAD
RIVER BANK
A3050

Start

Hampton Court Palace

HAMPTON COURT PARK

Hampton Court Palace

HAMPTON COURT

BRIDGE ROAD
CREEK ROAD
B3379

Hampton Court

HAMPTON COURT WAY

RIVER

THAMES

Ditton Field

HAMPTON COURT PALACE GOLF COURSE

A309

SUMMER ROAD

SPEER ROAD

Grist Memorial Sports Ground

Lee Valley White Water Centre
29 July – 2 August

Travelling to Lee Valley

✈ London Stansted Airport is 35km from Lee Valley White Water Centre, and has superb London connections. The Stansted Express is a 45 minute Rail link to London. Tel: 0844 335 1803.

⇄ Trains run regularly between Liverpool Street station in central London and Cheshunt stations, via Tottenham Hale in north-east London. Cheshunt station is a 20-minute walk to the Lee Valley White Water Centre.

Scan for Lee Valley Regional Park

♿ Accessibility

Assistance arrangements at London Stansted Airport must be booked through your airline at least 48 hours before your flight.

Cheshunt railway station is step-free with assistance available.

Shuttle buses for people with accessibility needs will run between Cheshunt station and the venue's entrance.

Visitor Highlights
☆

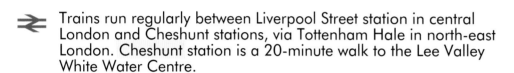

Waltham Abbey Church
Fine Norman Abbey founded in 1060 by King Harold.

Capel Manor Gardens
Enjoy the stunning scenery, picnic by the lake or relax in the restaurant.

Epping Forest
Epping Forest is the largest public open space in the London area, at almost 6,000 acres.

TURNFORD

A10

GT. CAMBRIDGE RD.
A1170

B176

HIGH RD TURNFORD

ST. LEONARDS
ROAD

B194

HALFHIDE LANE

HALFHIDE LA.

B156

WASH

HILL

GALLEYHILL WOOD

WEST LANE

CHESHUNT

River Lee Navigation

ROAD MARSH

B156

BROOKFIELD

HIGH STREET

B176

CHESHUNT

Aimes
Green

FLAMSTEAD ORD RD.

CAMBRIDGE

TURNER'S

CROSSBROOK

Holyfield

HOLYFIELD

Flamstead
End

CHURCHGATE RD.

HILL

B176

CROOKED

Fishers
Green

B194

CHESHUNT
&

A10

COLLEGE

B198

ROAD

CHESHUNT

LEE VALLEY
REGIONAL PARK

MILE

ROAD

HIGH

THEOBALDS
GROVE
&

Bowyer's
Water

River Lee Navigation

Horsemill Stream

Old River Lee

Royal
Gunpowder
Mills

VIEW

B198

ELLIS WAY

TENANT

GREAT

WINSTON

CHURCHILL WAY

A121

Lee Valley
White Water
Centre

B194

ABBEY

Waltham Abbey
Church

A10

CAMBRIDGE

ST. MONARCHS WY.

WALTHAM CROSS

ELEANOR CROSS ROAD

STATION ROAD

HIGHBRIDGE ST.

MERIDIAN

WALTHAM ABBEY

A1010

MONARCHS WY.

A121

WALTHAM
CROSS
&

Holdbrook

Town
Mead

Junction 25

Holmesdale
Tunnel

RD.

A1010

M25 MOTORWAY

A121

GREAT

M25

BULLSMOOR

A1055

LANE

HERTFORD

MOLLISON AVENUE

M25 MOTORWAY

A121

Bullsmoor

A1055

A10

ROAD

AVENUE

Gunpowder Park

WAY

ROAD

A121

TURKEY
STREET
&

Freezy
Water

ENFIELD
LOCK
&

SEWARDSTONE

Enfield
Lock

Enfield Island
Village

A112

A1010

Enfield
Wash

MOLLISON

A1055

field
hway

Scale:

0   500 m

Brimsdown

King George's
Reservoir

Sewardstone

67

Lee Valley White Water Centre

29 July – 2 August

The Lee Valley White Water Centre, located in Hertfordshire, will host the Canoe Slalom competition during the London 2012 Olympic Games.

Two new canoe slalom courses have been built, a 300m competition course and a 160m intermediate/training course.

Getting to the Venue

There are local bus routes and stops which provide access to this venue.

P+R There are park-and-ride locations in the area that will serve this venue.

The venue is a pleasant 20-minute walk from Cheshunt station. The route is flat and off-road and follows the Lee Valley Pathway through the Lee Valley Regional Park.

Free, secure, managed cycle parking will be provided to the north-east of the venue. The venue is on the Lee Valley Pathway within the Lee Valley Regional Park. It is also located on the National Cycle Network route 1 and 61.

A taxi drop-off point will be provided at Highbridge retail park, directly south of the venue. This is approximately five minutes walk from the venue's entrance.

An accessible shuttle will be provided to the venue from Cheshunt station and Highbridge retail park.

Limited, pre-booked parking will be provided close to the venue for disabled spectators who are UK Blue Badge holders or members of an equivalent national scheme.

• • • • Recommended spectator access routes to and from the venue.

Venue entrance or exit.

Scan for the latest transport information

Canoe Slalom

Canoe Slalom competitions consist of timed runs down a white water course, which contains up to 25 gates.

Touching a gate adds a two-second time penalty to the run; missing a gate incurs a 50-second penalty.

Thistly Marsh

to: CHESHUNT

Scale:
0   100 m

Hall Marsh

BOWYER'S WATER

OLD RIVER LEA or LEE

ROYAL GUNPOWDER MILLS

Small River Lea or Lee

RIVER LEE NAVIGATION

HORSEMILL STREAM

Royal Gunpowder Mills

LEE VALLEY
REGIONAL PARK

Waltham Marsh

Cheshunt
Marsh

**Lee Valley
White Water Centre**

P+R

WALTHAM
ABBEY

WALTHAM
CROSS

HIGHBRIDGE ST.

HIGHBRIDGE
ST. B194

HIGHBRIDGE
RETAIL PARK

A121   CROSS   ROAD   STATION   ROAD

MERIDIAN

Hazelmere
Marina

LEANOR

A121 CROSS

WALTHAM
CROSS

School

A121

Town Mead

Holdbrook

M25

M25

M25 MOTORWAY

WAY

Wembley

Stadium 29 July – 11 August
Arena 28 July – 12 August

Wembley is in north-west London, around six miles from the city centre.

Scan for Wembley Arena

Travelling to Wembley

Heathrow airport is 23km from Wembley and has superb London connections. The London Underground Piccadilly Line runs from all Terminals.

There are two recommended National Rail stations which provide access to Wembley Arena: Wembley Stadium station, with direct services from Marylebone station in central London, the Chilterns and Birmingham, and Wembley Central station, with direct train services from Euston station in central London.

Scan for Wembley Stadium

 ## Accessibility

Heathrow Airport has facilities for passengers with reduced mobility. Telephone +44 (0)844 335 1801.

Wembley Stadium station and Wembley Park station are step-free with staff assistance available.

Visitor Highlights

RAF museum Hendon

The only London attraction to house over 100 aircraft from around the world. Free admission plus free interactive and fun activities.

Kenwood House

Visit Kenwood House in London and discover world-famous art collections in fashionable Hampstead.

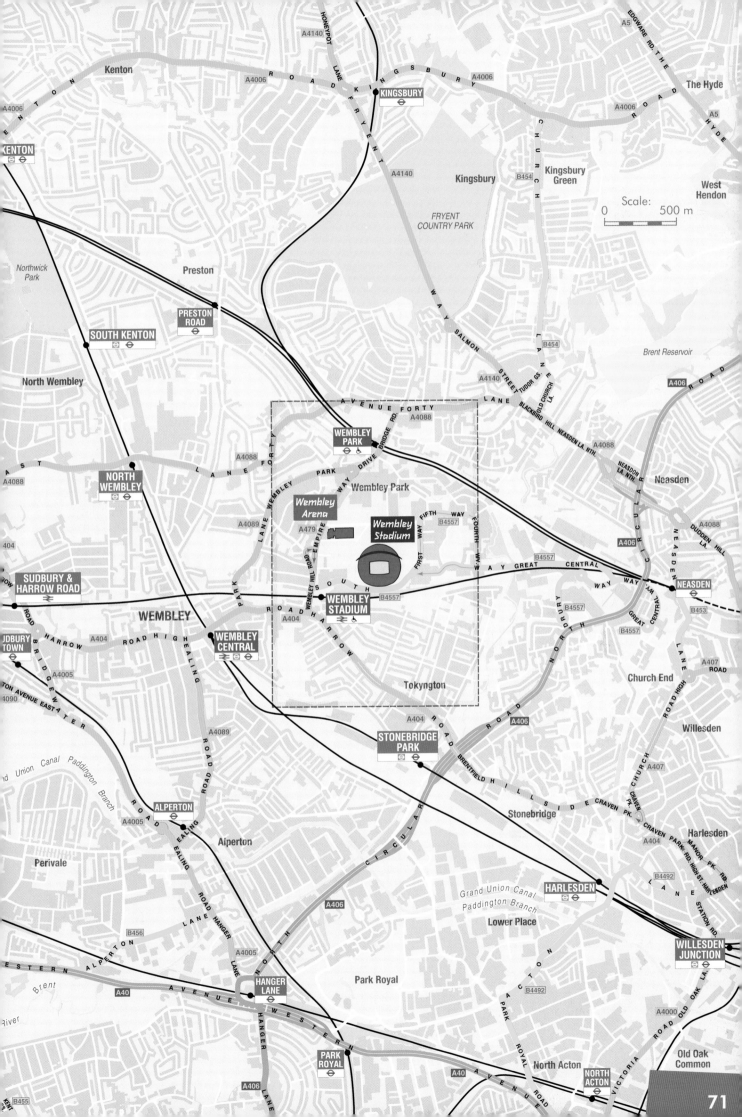

Kenton

A4140 HONEYPOT LANE

A4006

ROAD

A4006

KINGSBURY

A4006

LANE KINGSBURY

A5 EDGWARE RD THE

The Hyde

A5 HYDE

West Hendon

KENTON

A4006

Kingsbury

B454

Kingsbury Green

A4140

FRYENT COUNTRY PARK

Scale:
0   500 m

Northwick Park

Preston

PRESTON ROAD

A4140

WAY SALMON STREET

CHURCH LANE

B454

OLD CHURCH LA.

TUDOR GS.

BLACKBIRD HILL NEASDEN LA. NTH.

A4088

NEASDEN LA. NTH.

Brent Reservoir

SOUTH KENTON

North Wembley

A4088 LANE FORTY

AVENUE FORTY

A4088

WEMBLEY PARK

BRIDGE RD

A4088

Neasden

A4088

DUDDEN HILL LA.

EAST

A4088

NORTH WEMBLEY

A4089

LANE WEMBLEY

PARK WAY

DRIVE

Wembley Park

Wembley Arena

A479

Wembley Stadium

FIFTH WAY

WAY

B4557

FOURTH WAY

A406

A406 CIRCULAR

404

EMPIRE

WAY

FIRST WAY GREAT CENTRAL

B4557

SUDBURY & HARROW ROAD

WEMBLEY

ROAD HARROW

A404

WEMBLEY HILL ROAD

SOUTH

WEMBLEY STADIUM

B4557

B4557

NEASDEN

B453

JDBURY TOWN

ROAD HARROW

A404

ROAD HIGH EALING

WEMBLEY CENTRAL

NORBURY ROAD

B4557

WAY GREAT CENTRAL

Church End

ROAD HIGH

A407 ROAD

BRIDGE

A4005

EASTWATER

TON AVENUE EAST

A4090

Tokyngton

Willesden

ROAD

A4089 EALING

A406

ROAD

A406

STONEBRIDGE PARK

BRENTFIELD

HILLSIDE

CRAVEN PK.

Stonebridge

CHURCH

A404

ROAD HIGH ST. HARLESDEN

MANOR PK.

CRAVEN PARK RD.

Harlesden

B4492

nd Union Canal Paddington Branch

ROAD

ALPERTON

A4005

LANE HANGER

Alperton

Perivale

B456

ALPERTON

EALING

A406

Park Royal

A4005

CIRCULAR

Grand Union Canal Paddington Branch

HARLESDEN

Lower Place

STATION RD.

LANE

WILLESDEN JUNCTION

Brent River

A40

ESTERN AVENUE

HANGER LANE

HANGER

HANGER LANE

AVENUE WESTERN

PARK ROYAL

ROAD

ROYAL

ACTON

PARK

B4492

A40

VICTORIA

ROAD OLD OAK LA.

A4000

North Acton

Old Oak Common

A406

PARK ROYAL

AVENUE

NORTH ACTON

71

Wembley

Stadium 29 July – 11 August
Arena 28 July – 12 August

Getting to the Venues

There are two recommended London Underground stations which provide access to Wembley Stadium: Wembley Park on the Jubilee and Metropolitan lines; and Wembley Central on the Bakerloo line.

Wembley Central is on the London Overground line between Euston and Watford Junction.

London has an extensive bus network and there are routes and stops in the area.

Sections 9 and 10 of the Capital Ring, which offers some of London's best views, are approximately 4kms north-west of the venue.

Free, secure, managed cycle parking will be provided at or near the venue.

The taxi rank is located outside Wembley Park station on Bridge Road.

Limited, pre-booked parking will be provided close to the venue for disabled spectators who are UK Blue Badge holders or members of an equivalent national scheme.

• • • • Recommended spectator access routes to and from the venue.

Venue entrance or exit.

Scan for the latest transport information

Football

Extra time: If a match in the knockout stages is tied at the end of 90 minutes, the teams play 30 minutes of extra time in a bid to find a winner.

Badminton

Matches are played over the best of three games, and each game is won by the first player or doubles pair to reach 21 points by a margin of two clear points.

Gymnastics Rhythmic

One of the most beautiful spectacles on the Olympic programme.

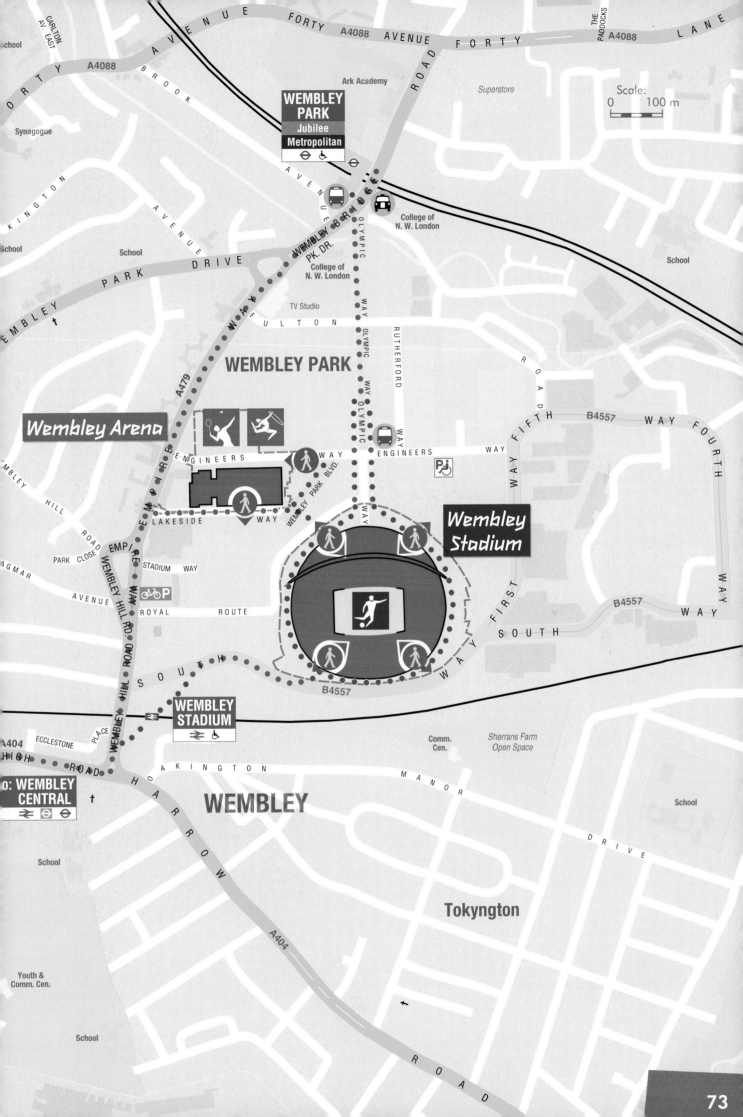

Wimbledon - London
28 July - 5 August

Wimbledon is the home of the All England Lawn Tennis and Croquet Club and the setting for the famous Wimbledon tennis tournament since 1877.

Travelling to Wimbledon

✈ Heathrow airport is 24km from the venue and has superb London connections. The Heathrow Express is a 15 minute non-stop link to London Paddington.

🚆 Wimbledon station is 2km from the venue. The station has direct services from London Waterloo, the south coast and Exeter, with connections from the rest of the National Rail network. Rail services from London Waterloo to Wimbledon take 10 minutes.

🚋 The popular London tram network runs from Wimbledon through Croydon to Beckenham.

♿ Accessibility

Heathrow Airport has facilities for passengers with reduced mobility. Telephone +44 (0)844 335 1801.

Wimbledon station is step-free with staff assistance available.

Scan for
www.Wimbledon.com

Visitor Highlights

Hampton Court Palace

Discover some of Hampton Courts sights and stories, these include The Great Hall, The Royal Chapel, Gardens and Maze.

Royal Botanic Gardens, Kew

Explore glasshouses, landscapes and 250 years of history at the world's most famous garden. Climb to the treetops, delve into rainforest or discover more on a guided tour.

Wimbledon - Lawn Tennis Club
28 July - 5 August

The Tennis competition at London 2012 will be held on the grass courts of Wimbledon, which has its own Olympic history. The venue staged the Tennis competition when London first hosted the Olympic Games in 1908, with Great Britain winning all six gold medals.

Getting to the Venue

  There are two recommended London Underground stations close to the venue: Wimbledon and Southfields on the District line. Both stations are step-free with staff assistance.

 Shuttle buses will run from Wimbledon station to the venue.

 London has an extensive bus network and there are routes and stops in the area.

 Section 6 of the Capital Ring goes from Wimbledon Park to Richmond Bridge. There are lots of other walking routes in the area.

 Free, secure, managed cycle parking will be provided near the venue.

 There will be a taxi and private hire vehicle drop-off point close to the venue.

 Limited, pre-booked parking will be provided close to the venue for disabled spectators who are UK Blue Badge holders or members of an equivalent national scheme.

• • • • Recommended spectator access routes to and from the venue.

◀(🚶)▶ Venue entrance or exit.

 Scan for the latest transport information

Tennis

Tennis appeared at the first modern Olympic Games in 1896 but was dropped from the programme after the Paris 1924 Games. It returned 64 years later at Seoul 1988.

The first tennis balls were made of wool or hair, wrapped up in leather.

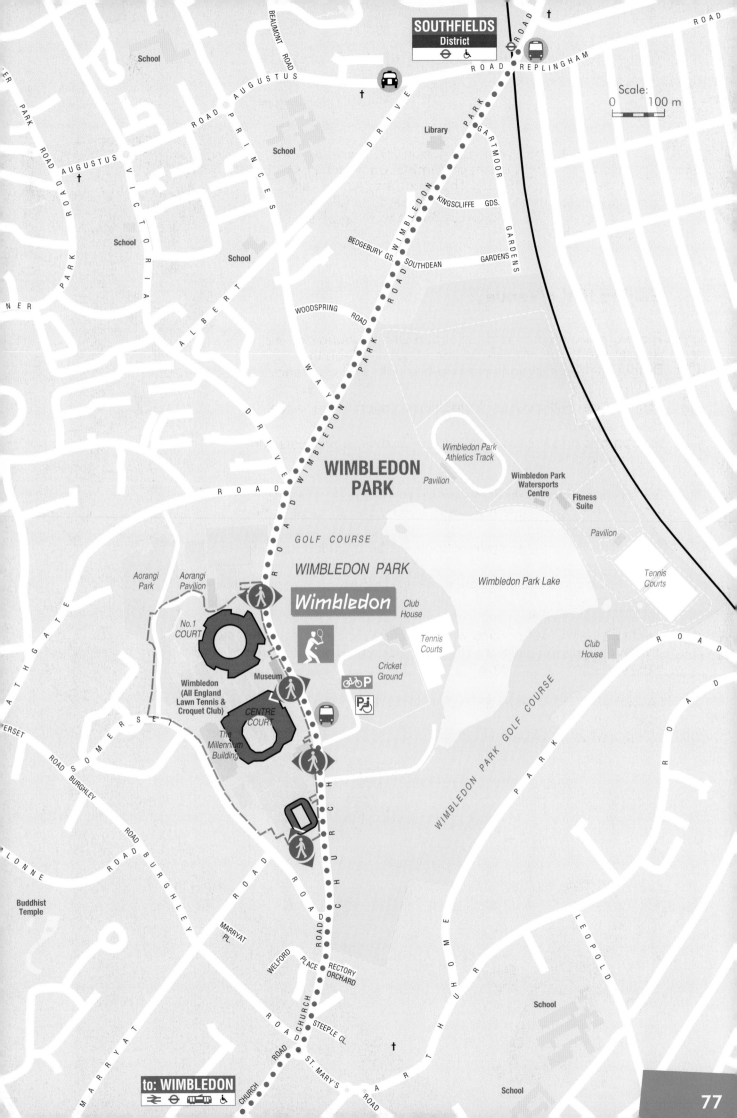

Scale:
0   100 m

School

ROAD AUGUSTUS

BEAUMONT ROAD

School

PARK ROAD

ROAD AUGUSTUS

VICTORIA PARK

PRINCES

School

School

ALBERT DRIVE

Library

ROAD REPLINGHAM

ROAD

WIMBLEDON PARK ROAD

GARTMOOR GARDENS

KINGSCLIFFE GDS.

BEDGEBURY GS.

SOUTHDEAN GARDENS

WOODSPRING ROAD

WAY

WIMBLEDON
PARK

Pavilion

Wimbledon Park
Athletics Track

Wimbledon Park
Watersports
Centre

Fitness
Suite

Pavilion

GOLF COURSE

WIMBLEDON PARK

Wimbledon Park Lake

Tennis
Courts

DRIVE

ROAD

Aorangi
Park

Aorangi
Pavilion

No.1
COURT

Wimbledon

Club
House

Tennis
Courts

Club
House

Museum

Wimbledon
(All England
Lawn Tennis &
Croquet Club)

CENTRE
COURT

Cricket
Ground

WIMBLEDON PARK GOLF COURSE

ROAD

The
Millennium
Building

SOMERSET ROAD

PARK

ROAD

LEOPOLD ROAD

ROAD BURGHLEY

CHURCH ROAD

ARTHUR ROAD

ROAD

Buddhist
Temple

MARRYAT ROAD

ROAD BURGHLEY

MARRYAT
PL.

WELFORD ROAD

PLACE

RECTORY
ORCHARD

School

School

ONNE

STEEPLE CL.

ST. MARY'S ROAD

CHURCH ROAD

School

Beijing 2008 Olympic Games
Sergio Aguero of Argentina is challenged by
Breno of Brazil during the men's football semifinal
match between Argentina and Brazil

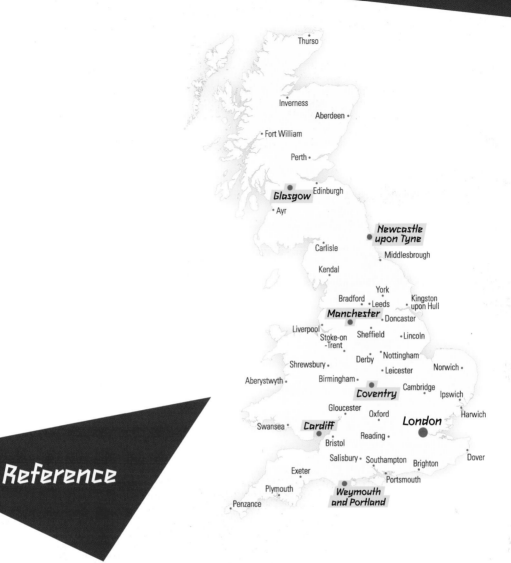

Reference

Motorway — M25
Primary route — A12
A road — A118 | A118
B road — B112 | B112
One way
Airport —
Rail — Stations | Tunnel
Tram — Stations | Tunnel
Station names — VICTORIA
Recommended stations — WEMBLEY
Step-free station
National rail
Overground

Underground
DLR — DLR
Tram — Metrolink / Tramlink
Metro (Newcastle) — M
Subway (Glasgow) — S
Riverboat — Recommended Stop — WESTMINSTER
Bus
Coach
Shuttle bus
Taxi
Cycle parking — P
Park and ride — P+R — Pick up / Drop off
Blue Badge parking — P

Spectator route — • • • •
Entrance and exit
Live Site — LS
Venue perimeter
Visitor highlights — ★
Venue name — The Mall
Venue building
Olympic sport
Paralympic sport
Built up area
Parks and rivers

Coventry   25 July - 9 August

The City of Coventry is ideally located in the centre of England. Confirmed as a London 2012 Live Site venue, a big screen will be installed at the Coventry Transport Museum.

Travelling to Coventry

 Birmingham Airport is located approximately 26 km from the City of Coventry Stadium. There are regular train connections from Birmingham International railway station to Coventry railway station.

 Coventry station is the closest National Rail station to the venue. The station has direct train services from London, north-west England and the south coast, Birmingham and throughout the West Midlands, with connections from the rest of the National Rail network.

♿ Accessibility

Birmingham Airport has facilities for passengers with reduced mobility. To arrange this please contact your airline or tour operator at least 48 hours before departure/arrival.

Coventry station is step-free with staff assistance available.

 London 2012 Live Site, Coventry Transport Museum.

Scan for visit Coventry and Warwickshire

Visitor Highlights

☆ Coventry Cathedral (St. Michael's)

Today the ruins of the old Cathedral are preserved as a memorial and sacred space for the City.

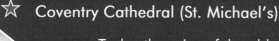

Warwick castle

This imposing Medieval castle, built by William the Conqueror in 1068, was used as a fortification until the early 17th century.

Scale:
0 — 500 m

M6
A444
Exhall
Junction 3
B4113
Canal
Ash Green
Coventry Canal
Hawkesbury
Keresley Newland
PICKARDS WAY
B4109
GROVE
M6
Neal's Green
A444
LONGFORD WAY
M6 MOTORWAY
Oxford Canal
Foxford
ROAD PARROTTS
BEDWORTH ROAD
Rowleys Green
PHOENIX WAY
Longford
Alderman's Green
City of Coventry Stadium
B4113
Longford Park
ALDERMAN'S GREEN
Holbrooks
ROAD LONGFORD
B4109
KERESLEY
Hall Green
HALL GREEN
ROAD HENLEY
Little Heath
B4082
ROAD
Whitmore Park
OLD FOLESHILL
CHURCH
PHOENIX WAY
Wood End
HOLBROOK WAY
A444
Foleshill
GREEN ROAD
KERESLEY
B4098
HOLBROOK LA.
B4118
LOCKHURST LANE
B4113
Coventry Canal
BELL GREEN ROAD
B4109
Bell Green
B4082
ROAD
Edgwick
River Sowe
ROAD RADFORD
Radford
STANTON LANE
Great Heath
Paradise
Court House Green
A444 WAY
Wyken Green
AVENUE ENGLETON RD.
FOLESHILL LANE
B4109
Stoke Heath
B4107
B4098
B4113
Bishopsgate Green
B4110 EAST
PHOENIX WAY
Upper Stoke
Wyken
N HARNALL LANE
SWAN LANE
A4600
ROAD ANSTY
YHEAD MOSELEY
Draper's Field
A444
ROAD
A4114
HOLYHEAD ROAD
RINGWAY ST. NICHOLAS
1
RINGWAY SWANSWELL
Hillfields
WALSGRAVE ROAD
B4107
9
RINGWAY HILL CROSS
BIRDS WHITE ST.
2
HOBGRAVE ROAD
A4053
SWANSWELL ST.
Middle Stoke
8
LS
A444
BINLEY
A4106
ESLEY OLD RD.
SPON END BUTTS
7
Coventry Transport Museum
3
RINGWAY WHITEFRIARS
SKY BLUE WAY
A4600
BINLEY RD.
KINGSWAY
A428
Spon End
★
Coventry Cathedral
SWAN LANE
HUMBER
ROAD
Stoke
RINGWAY RUDGE
COVENTRY
Gosford Green
Lower Stoke
RSALL LANE
B4101
ROAD
A4053
4
B4101
5
RINGWAY QUEENS
RINGWAY ST. JOHNS
LONDON ROAD
B4110
A4082
B4107
6
RINGWAY ST. PATRICKS
A4114
AV. NTH.
RD.
COVENTRY 🚉
WARWICK RD.
A429

81

City of Coventry Stadium
25 July - 9 August

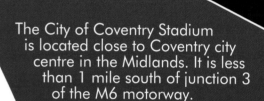

The stadium was opened officially by Dame Kelly Holmes on 24 February 2007, and will play host to 12 Football matches during the Games, including the women's Bronze medal match.

Getting to the Venue

🚌 Shuttle buses will run from Coventry train station to the venue.

🚍 There are local bus routes and stops that provide access to this venue.

P+R There will be park-and-ride sites serving this venue during the Games.

♿P Limited, pre-booked parking will be provided for disabled spectators who are UK Blue Badge holders or members of an equivalent national scheme.

🚕 There will be a taxi and private hire vehicle pick-up/drop-off point close to the venue.

🚲P Free, secure, managed cycle parking will be provided at the venue.

🚶 The City of Coventry Stadium is over one hour's walk from the closest National Rail station and the town centre.

•••• Recommended spectator access routes to and from the venue.

◀🚶▶ Venue entrance or exit.

The City of Coventry Stadium is located close to Coventry city centre in the Midlands. It is less than 1 mile south of junction 3 of the M6 motorway.

It is approximately 140km north west of London.

Scan for the latest transport information

Football

Penalty shootout: If the scores are tied at the end of extra time, there's a penalty shootout, in which each team has five penalty kicks. If the teams remain tied after five penalties, the shootout takes a sudden-death form, with single rounds of one kick per team to determine the winner.

Scale
0   100 m

eal's
reen

PICKARDS B4113
WAY
M6
M6 MOTORWAY
LONGFORD ROAD

A444

LANE

ROAD
B4113

WILSONS

WOODSHIRES

ROAD OBAN

ROAD

ROAD BEDWORTH

Coventry Welsh
Rugby Football
Ground

PHOENIX

Rowleys
Green

Longford

LANE

OAKMOOR   ROAD

RBAGES

DING
HOUSE
PINGTON
LANE
DRIVE
ALDER
MDW. CL.
LAUDERDALE

LANE

ROWLEYS GREEN

ROWLEY'S GN. JUDD'S
LA.

LANE

PHOENIX

**City of Coventry
Stadium**

LANE
GREEN

LONGFORD PARK

AVENUE

P

A444

PHOENIX

WAY

School

COVENTRY CANAL

B4113

LONGFORD

ROAD

CLASSIC DR.

ARENA
RETAIL PARK

WINDMILL   ROAD

BEDLAM
LANE

YTHALLS

BARTLETT
CL.
LANE

ELMSDALE AV. ARBURY

AVENUE

FOLESHILL

Sikh
Temple

Foleshill
Cemetery

Little Heath

Travelling to Glasgow

 Glasgow Airport is located approximately 16Km from the Hampden Park venue, and offers up to 58 flights a day to London. Tel: 0844 481 5555.

 The recommended station for Hampden Park is Mount Florida, which is 400m from the venue. The station has direct services from Glasgow Central, with connections to the rest of the National Rail network.

(S) Subway system provides easy access around the city centre.

♿ Accessibility

Glasgow Airport has facilities for passengers with reduced mobility. You must inform your airline of your particular need at least 48 hours before you fly.

Mount Florida station has a step-free route from one entrance to both platforms and staff assistance is available.

Glasgow is approximately 670km north of London.

National Rail services take around 4.5 hours from London Euston to Glasgow.

Glasgow Rail & Subway Connections.

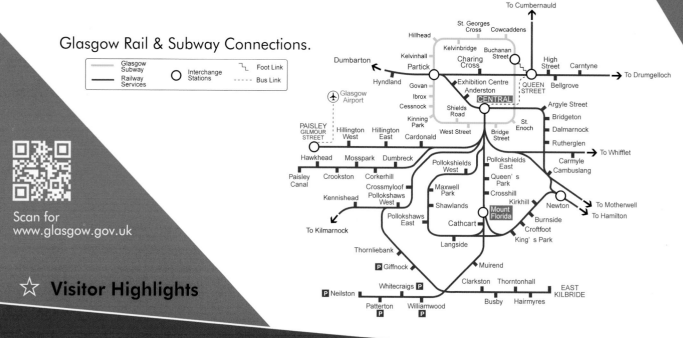

Scan for
www.glasgow.gov.uk

☆ Visitor Highlights

Glasgow Science Centre

Glasgow Science Centre is one of Scotland's must-see visitor attractions-presenting concepts of science and technology in unique and inspiring ways.

Kelvingrove Art Gallery & Museum

One of Scotland's most popular free attractions with state-of-the-art galleries displaying an astonishing 8000 objects.

Hampden Park, Glasgow

25 July - 3 August

Hampden Park is Scotland's national football stadium. It is also used for music concerts and other sporting events.

The stadium will host a total of eight Olympic Football matches, with action in both the men's and women's competitions.

Getting to the Venue

🚌 There are local bus routes and stops that provide access to this venue.

🚐 A shuttle service will run from central Glasgow (Buchanan Street) to the venue.

P+R There will be park-and-ride sites serving this venue during the Games.

P♿ Limited, pre-booked parking will be provided for disabled spectators who are UK Blue Badge holders or members of an equivalent national scheme.

🚕 There will be a taxi and private hire vehicle drop-off point close to the venue.

🚲P Free, secure, managed cycle parking will be provided at the venue.

🚶 Glasgow city centre is approximately one hour from Hampden Park by foot.

• • • • Recommended spectator access routes to and from the venue.

◀(🚶)▶ Venue entrance or exit.

Scan for the latest transport information

Football

The Football competition at London 2012 will be staged at six grounds around the UK.

• Indirect free kick: A type of free kick from which the attacking team cannot score directly without more than one player touching the ball first.

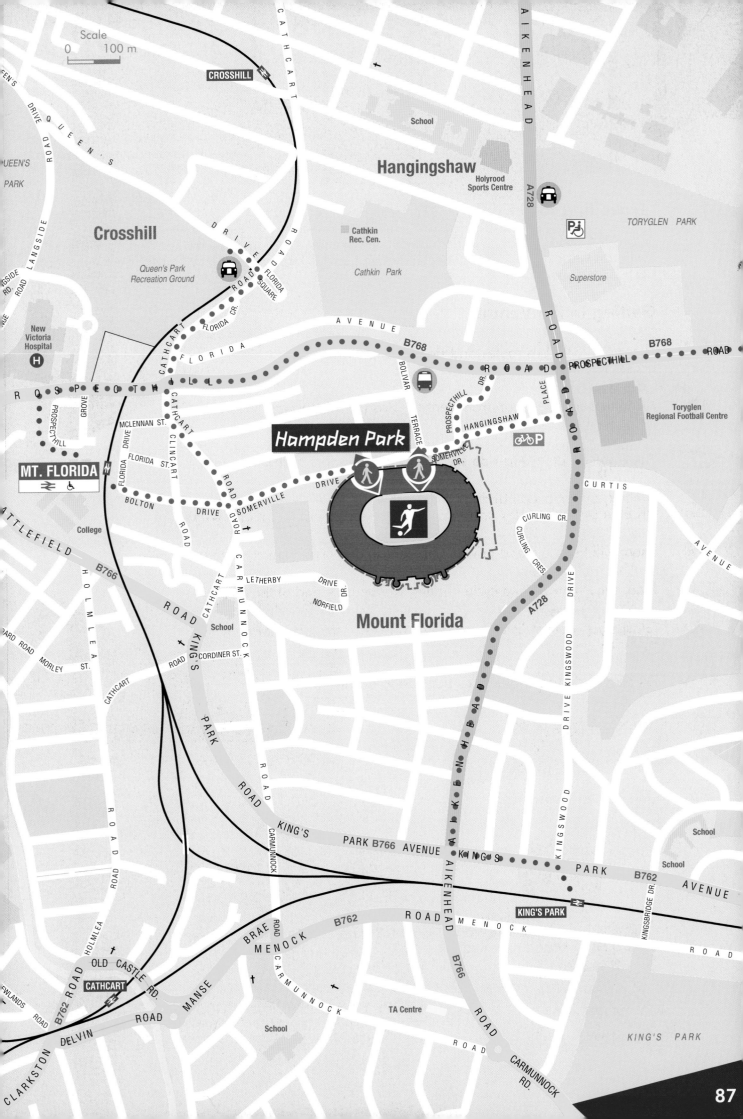

Scale
0   100 m

CROSSHILL

Crosshill

Queen's Park
Recreation Ground

QUEEN'S
PARK

QUEEN'S ROAD

LANGSIDE ROAD

New Victoria
Hospital
H

PROSPECTHILL

PROSPECTHILL

ROSPECTHILL

GROVE

MCLENNAN ST.

FLORIDA DRIVE

FLORIDA ST.

MT. FLORIDA

BOLTON DRIVE

College

ATTLEFIELD

B766

HOLMLEA ROAD

BOARD ROAD MORLEY ST.

CATHCART ROAD

KING'S PARK ROAD

CORDINER ST.

CARMUNNOCK ROAD

School

LETHERBY

NORFIELD DR.

DRIVE

Mount Florida

CATHCART ROAD

CLINCART ROAD

SOMERVILLE ROAD

SOMERVILLE DRIVE

DRIVE

Hampden Park

School

Hangingshaw

Holyrood
Sports Centre

Cathkin
Rec. Cen.

Cathkin Park

AVENUE

B768

BOLIVAR

ROAD

PROSPECTHILL

B768 ROAD

PROSPECTHILL DR.

HANGINGSHAW

PLACE

TERRACE

SOMERVILLE DR.

CURTIS AVENUE

CURLING CR.

CURLING CRES.

A728

AIKENHEAD ROAD

A728

School

TORYGLEN PARK

Superstore

Toryglen
Regional Football Centre

KINGSWOOD DRIVE

KINGSWOOD DRIVE

KING'S PARK B766 AVENUE

KING'S PARK B762 AVENUE

KINGSBRIDGE DR.

KING'S PARK

ROAD

B762 ROAD

HOLMLEA ROAD

OLD CASTLE RD.

CATHCART

EWLANDS ROAD

CLARKSTON DELVIN ROAD

MANSE

BRAE MENOCK ROAD

B762 MENOCK CARMUNNOCK ROAD

School

TA Centre

CARMUNNOCK RD.

AIKENHEAD ROAD B766

MENOCK ROAD

KING'S PARK

ROAD

School

School

The Millennium Stadium is located on the banks of the River Taff, right in the heart of the Welsh capital, Cardiff. It is just three hours away from the centre of London by road or two hours by rail.

Travelling to Cardiff

✈ Cardiff Airport, 19 kms west of Cardiff city centre, is the gateway for connecting Wales with the world. A rail link connects Rhoose Cardiff Airport Station to Cardiff Central station. Tel: 01446 711111

🚆 Cardiff Central station is a five minute walk from the venue. There are direct trains from London Paddington, Birmingham, the south coast and south-west England, with connections from the rest of the National Rail network.

♿ Accessibility

Cardiff Airport has facilities for passengers with reduced mobility Tel: 01446 729329.

Cardiff Central station is step-free with staff assistance available. You will need to book this when you buy your train ticket.

Cardiff Millennium Centre

Cardiff Castle

★ Visitor Highlights

Cardiff Castle
Discover 2000 years of history in the heart of the city. From the arrival of the Romans, through the Norman Conquest to lavish Victorian design.

Wales Millennium Centre
Visitors come to enjoy blockbuster West End musicals, opera, ballet and contemporary dance, hip hop and stand up comedy and art exhibitions.

Cardiff Bay and Visitors Centre
Cardiff Bay is a hub of activity attracting crowds to its pretty waterfront setting, striking architecture and numerous trendy bars and restaurants.

www.visitcardiff.com

Millennium Stadium, Cardiff
25 July - 10 August

The Millennium Stadium has the honour of hosting the very first event of the Olympic Games, with women's Football matches starting on 25 July, two days before the Opening Ceremony.

The stadium will host 11 matches on eight separate dates finishing with the men's bronze medal match.

With a retractable roof and a capacity of 74,600, the Millennium Stadium has hosted many top sporting events, including FA Cup finals and the 1999 Rugby World Cup Final.

Since opening in June 1999, the stadium has welcomed, on average, 1.3 million visitors per year.

Getting to the Venue

Scan for the latest transport information

 There are local bus routes and stops that provide access to this venue.

 P+R There will be park-and-ride sites serving this venue during the Games.

 Limited, pre-booked parking will be provided for disabled spectators who are UK Blue Badge holders or members of an equivalent national scheme.

 There will be a taxi and private hire vehicle drop-off point close to the venue.

 Free, secure, managed cycle parking will be provided at the venue.

• • • • Recommended spectator access routes to and from the venue.

 Venue entrance or exit.

 London 2012 Live Site, The Hayes.

Football

Football was introduced as a medal sport at the 1908 Olympic Games. Great Britain won the gold medal, then successfully defended their title four years later in Stockholm.

• Advantage: Played by the referee after a foul if he feels that the team that has been fouled wouldn't benefit from a stoppage in play.

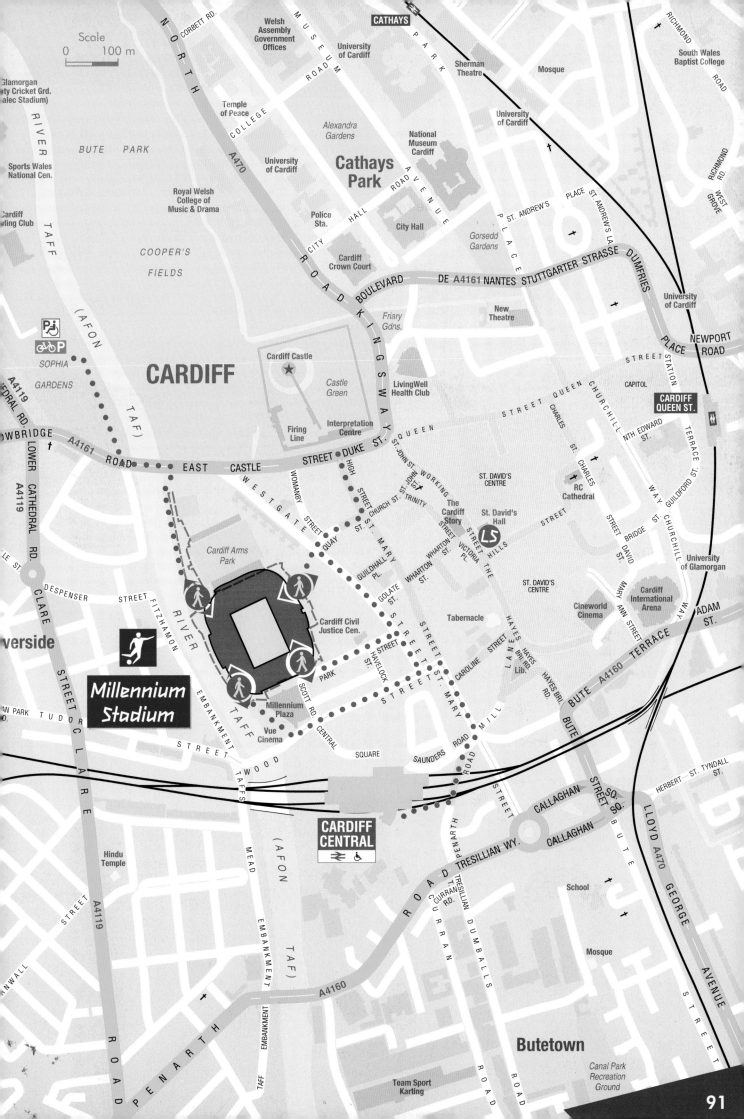

Scale
0   100 m

CORBETT RD.

NORTH ROAD A470

COLLEGE ROAD

MUSEUM AVENUE

Welsh Assembly Government Offices

University of Cardiff

PARK PLACE

Sherman Theatre

Mosque

RICHMOND ROAD

South Wales Baptist College

Glamorgan ~ty Cricket Grd. ~alec Stadium)

RIVER TAFF

BUTE PARK

Temple of Peace

Alexandra Gardens

University of Cardiff

National Museum Cardiff

University of Cardiff

RICHMOND RD.

WEST GROVE

Sports Wales National Cen.

Cardiff ~wling Club

COOPER'S FIELDS

Royal Welsh College of Music & Drama

CITY HALL ROAD

Police Sta.

City Hall

ST. ANDREW'S PLACE

ST. ANDREW'S LA.

DUMFRIES PLACE

University of Cardiff

NEWPORT ROAD

Gorsedd Gardens

Cardiff Crown Court

BOULEVARD DE A4161 NANTES STUTTGARTER STRASSE

STATION TERRACE

Friary Gdns.

New Theatre

STREET

CAPITOL

CARDIFF QUEEN ST.

P♿ 🚲P

SOPHIA GARDENS

Cardiff Castle

Castle Green

LivingWell Health Club

STREET QUEEN

CHARLES ST.

CHURCHILL WAY

NTH. EDWARD ST.

CHARLES ST.

~HEDRAL RD. A4119

~OWBRIDGE A4161 ROAD

EAST CASTLE STREET

Firing Line

DUKE ST.

Interpretation Centre

ST. JOHN ST.

ST. JOHN WORKING

QUEEN STREET

St. DAVID'S CENTRE

RC Cathedral

GUILDFORD ST.

LOWER CATHEDRAL RD. A4119

WESTGATE STREET

QUAY ST.

HIGH STREET

CHURCH ST. TRINITY ST.

The Cardiff Story

St. David's Hall

STREET THE HILLS

BRIDGE ST.

DAVID ST.

CHURCHILL WAY

~LE ST.

Cardiff Arms Park

ST. MARY ST.

WHARTON ST.

VICTORIA PL.

WHARTON ST.

St. DAVID'S CENTRE

MARY ANN STREET

University of Glamorgan

CLARE STREET

DESPENSER STREET

FITZHAMON EMBANKMENT

RIVER TAFF

GUILDHALL PL.

GOLATE ST.

Cardiff Civil Justice Cen.

Cineworld Cinema

Cardiff International Arena

ADAM ST.

~verside

🚶

🚶

Cardiff Civil Justice Cen.

🚶

Tabernacle

HAYES LANE

Hayes Bri. Rd.

Millennium Stadium

🚶

🚶

PARK STREET

HAVELOCK ST.

STREET ST. MARY

Lib.

HAYES BRI. RD.

BUTE TERRACE A4160

SCOTT RD.

Millennium Plaza

Vue Cinema

CENTRAL

CAROLINE STREET

MILL LANE

CLARE STREET

TUDOR STREET A4119

TAFF EMBANKMENT

WOOD STREET

SQUARE

SAUNDERS ROAD

ST. MARY ROAD

BUTE STREET

CALLAGHAN SQ.

CALLAGHAN SQ.

HERBERT ST.

TYNDALL ST.

LLOYD GEORGE AVENUE A470

Hindu Temple

MEAD EMBANKMENT

TAFFS

CARDIFF CENTRAL 🚄♿

PENARTH ROAD

CURRAN RD.

TRESILLIAN WY.

TRESILLIAN DUMBALLS ROAD

School

Mosque

PENARTH ROAD A4119

A4160

AFON TAF

CURRAN ROAD

Butetown

Canal Park Recreation Ground

Team Sport Karting

~NWALL STREET

CARDIFF

Travelling to Manchester

Manchester Airport is 13 kms south of Old Trafford Stadium, with fast transport links including the M60 and M56 Motorways. Manchester Airport offers more routes than any other UK airport serving 225 destinations across the World.

Manchester Piccadilly is 4km from Old Trafford Stadium. The station has direct services from London Euston, Birmingham and Glasgow, with connections from the rest of the National Rail network.

Greater Manchester's Metrolink network is one of the most successful light rail systems in the UK, carrying nearly 20 million passengers every year.

Accessibility

Manchester Airport has facilities for passengers with reduced mobility. Customer Service Tel: 08712 710 711

Manchester Piccadilly station is step-free with staff assistance available. You will need to book this when you buy your train ticket.

Scan for
visit Manchester

Manchester Rail & Metrolink Connections

Manchester Metrolink under construction	
Railway Services	
Interchange Stations	
Foot Link	

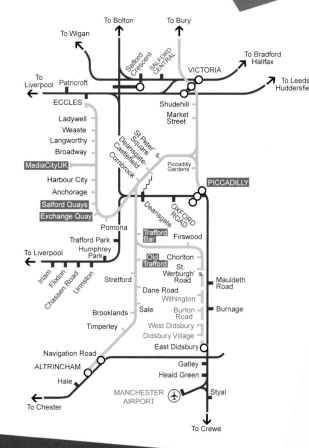

☆ **Visitor Highlights**

The Lowry

The Lowry Galleries showcase exhibitions by one of Britain's best loved artists, LS Lowry.

National Football Museum

The Museum provides a world-class home for the greatest collection of football memorabilia ever assembled.

Getting to the Venue

 The recommended Manchester Metrolink (tram) stations for the venue are Old Trafford, Trafford Bar, Exchange Quay, Salford Quays and Media City.

 All stations on the Manchester Metrolink network are step-free from entrance to vehicle.

 A shuttle service will run fron central Manchester (Piccadilly Gardens), to a location near the venue.

 There are local bus routes and stops that provide access to this venue.

 There is a boat service which stops close to the venue on Bridgewater Canal.

 There will be park-and-ride sites serving this venue during the Games.

 Limited, pre-booked parking will be provided for disabled spectators who are UK Blue Badge holders or members of an equivalent national scheme.

 There will be a taxi and private hire vehicle drop-off point close to the venue.

 Free, secure, managed cycle parking will be provided at the venue.

 There is a pedestrian walkway to Old Trafford from Manchester city centre. The walk is approximately 3.5 kilometres.

 Recommended spectator access routes to and from the venue.

 Venue entrance or exit.

 London 2012 Live Site, Exchange Square Manchester.

The 'Theatre of Dreams' is home to Manchester United Football Club. It first opened in 1910 and recently expanded to 76,000 seats.

It is the second largest football ground in the UK.

The Stadium will host nine football matches during the Olympic Games including a semi-final in both the men's and women's competitions.

 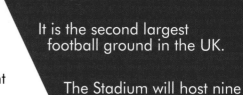 Scan for the latest transport information

Football

Each team may have 5 subs but can only use 3 during the game.

During the London 2012 Football competition, approximately 2,400 footballs will be used.

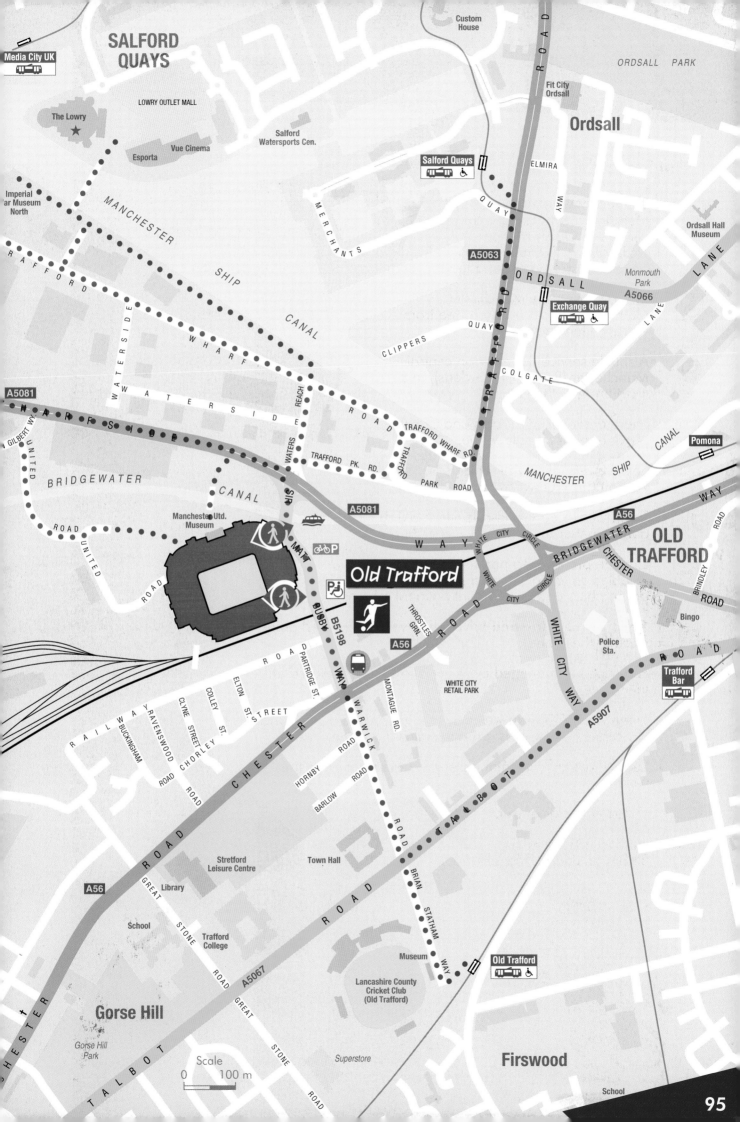

SALFORD QUAYS

Custom House

ORDSALL PARK

Media City UK

Ordsall

Fit City
Ordsall

LOWRY OUTLET MALL

ELMIRA

Salford
Watersports Cen.

Salford Quays

Ordsall Hall
Museum

The Lowry

Esporta

Vue Cinema

QUAY

A5063

WAY

LANE

MANCHESTER

M E R C H A N T S

ORDSALL

Monmouth
Park

Imperial
ar Museum
North

SHIP

Exchange Quay

A5066

LANE

RAFFORD

CANAL

CLIPPERS

COLGATE

QUAY

TRAFFORD

WATERSIDE

W A T E R S I D E

A5081

WHARF

REACH

ROAD

Trafford Wharf Rd.

Pomona

HARFSIDE

WATERS

Trafford
Park
Road

MANCHESTER

SHIP

CANAL

WAY

GILBERT WY.

BRIDGEWATER

TRAFFORD PK. RD.

CANAL

A5081

BRIDGEWATER

WAY

A56

OLD
TRAFFORD

UNITED

ROAD

Manchester Utd.
Museum

P

WHITE CITY CIRCLE

CHESTER

ROAD

ROAD

UNITED

Old Trafford

WHITE

CITY

CIRCLE

Brindley

Road

Bingo

P

CITY

WHITE

ROAD

BUSBY

B5198

A56

THROSTLES GRN.

Police
Sta.

Trafford Bar

WAY

ROAD

MONTAGUE RD.

WHITE CITY
RETAIL PARK

WHITE

CITY

WAY

A5907

RAILWAY

PARTRIDGE ST.

WARWICK

Old Trafford

ELTON

ST.

STREET

ROAD

CHORLEY

ST.

CLYNE STREET

COLLEY

HORNBY

ROAD

CHESTER

TALBOT

ROAD

BUCKINGHAM

RAVENSWOOD

ROAD

BARLOW

ROAD

ROAD

Stretford
Leisure Centre

Town Hall

BRIAN

STATHAM

A56

Library

GREAT

STONE

ROAD

A5067

Museum

WAY

Old Trafford

School

Trafford College

GREAT

STONE

ROAD

Lancashire County
Cricket Club
(Old Trafford)

Gorse Hill

Firswood

Gorse Hill
Park

Superstore

CHESTER

TALBOT

Scale

0   100 m

School

Newcastle 26 July - 4 August

Travelling to Newcastle-upon-Tyne

 Newcastle International Airport is located approximately 10kms from the city centre, and offers fifteen flights a day to London.
Tel: 0871 882 1121

Newcastle Central station is 600m from the venue. The station has direct services from London King's Cross, Birmingham and Edinburgh.

M There are four city centre Metro stations close to the venue – Haymarket, St. James, Monument and Central.

Accessibility

Newcastle International Airport has facilities for passengers with reduced mobility.

Newcastle station is step-free with assistance available.
All stations on the Newcastle Metro are step-free from entrance to vehicle.

St. James' Park is home to Newcastle United Football Club.

The stadium is situated in the centre of Newcastle-upon-Tyne in the north east of England.

Tyne & Wear Metro & Rail Connections

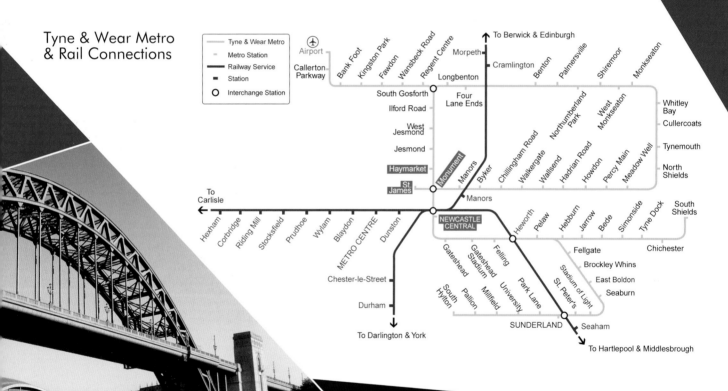

★ Visitor Highlights

Tyne Bridge
The most celebrated of all the Tyne's bridges.

The Sage Gateshead
The Sage is both a live music venue and a centre for musical education.

Baltic Centre for Contemporary Art
Visitors can experience innovative and provocative new art and discover fresh ideas.

www.newcastlegateshead.com

96

St. James' Park is 425kms outside London, but Newcastle-upon-Tyne is well served by National Rail from locations around the country and has a Metro system for easy travel around the city.

Getting to the Venue

 There are local bus routes and stops that provide access to this venue.

 There will be park-and-ride sites serving the venue during the Olympic Games.

 Limited, pre-booked parking will be provided close to the venue for disabled spectators who are UK Blue Badge holders or members of an equivalent national scheme.

 There will be a taxi and private hire vehicle drop-off point close to the venue.

 Free, secure, managed cycle parking will be provided at the venue.

 St. James' Park is in the city centre and very easy to access by foot.

• • • • Recommended spectator access routes to and from the venue.

 Venue entrance or exit.

St. James' Park will host a total of nine matches, including a quarter-final in both the men's and women's competitions.

St. James' Park is the oldest and largest football stadium in the North East of England.

It is the sixth largest stadium in the UK.

 Scan for the latest transport information

Football

Football has featured at every Olympic Games since 1908, with the exception of Los Angeles 1932.

Foul: Illegal interference with an opposing player, such as tripping.

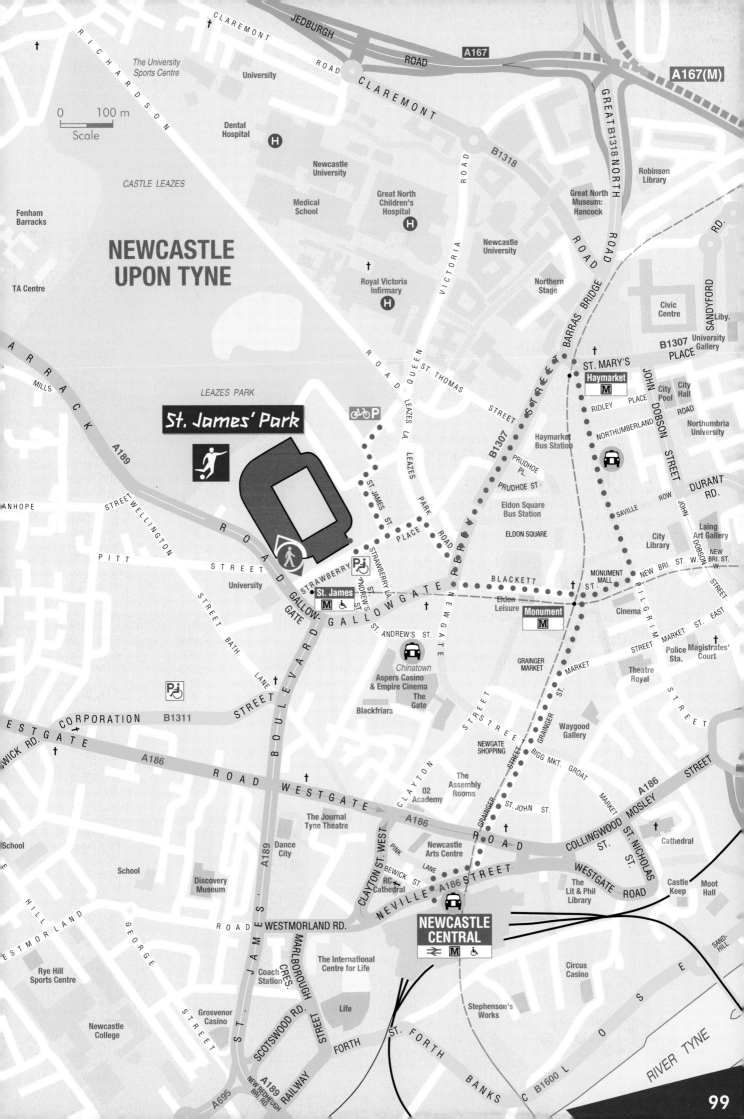

NEWCASTLE UPON TYNE

St. James' Park

Weymouth

29 July – 11 August

1 – 6 September

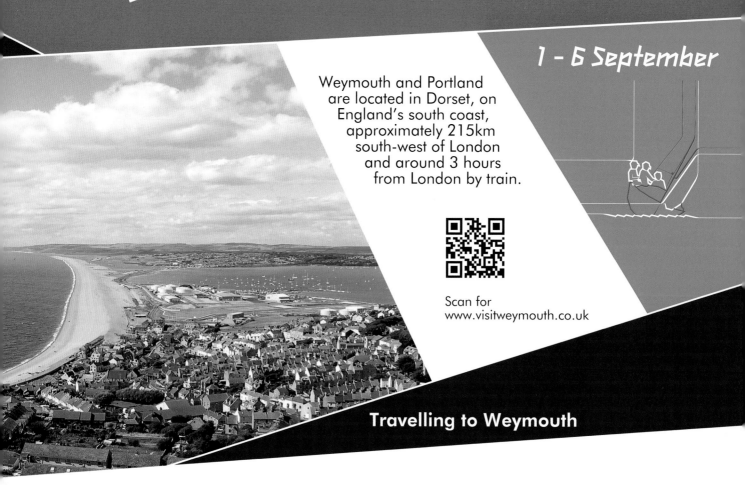

Weymouth and Portland are located in Dorset, on England's south coast, approximately 215km south-west of London and around 3 hours from London by train.

Scan for
www.visitweymouth.co.uk

Travelling to Weymouth

✈ Bournemouth Airport is located 58 kms east of Weymouth. It offers regular flights to many UK and European destinations, including Glasgow, Alderney, Amsterdam and Madrid.

⇄ Weymouth station is 2km from The Nothe and a short walk from Weymouth beach. The station has direct services from London Waterloo, the south coast, Bristol and Reading, with connections from the rest of the National Rail network.

♿ Accessibility

Bournemouth Airport's disability service provider can be contacted on Tel: 07534 988571.

Weymouth station is step-free with staff assistance available.

☆ Visitor Highlights

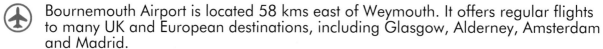

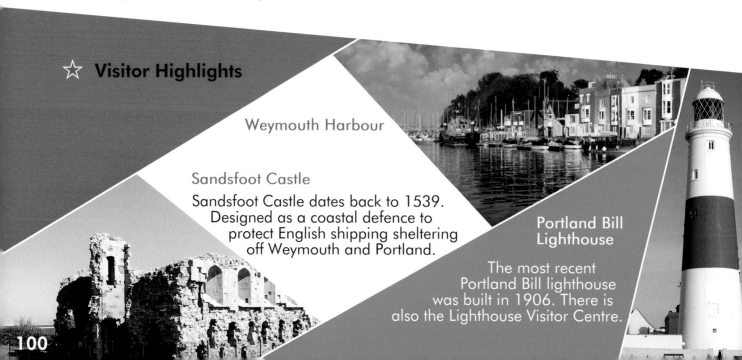

Weymouth Harbour

Sandsfoot Castle

Sandsfoot Castle dates back to 1539. Designed as a coastal defence to protect English shipping sheltering off Weymouth and Portland.

Portland Bill Lighthouse

The most recent Portland Bill lighthouse was built in 1906. There is also the Lighthouse Visitor Centre.

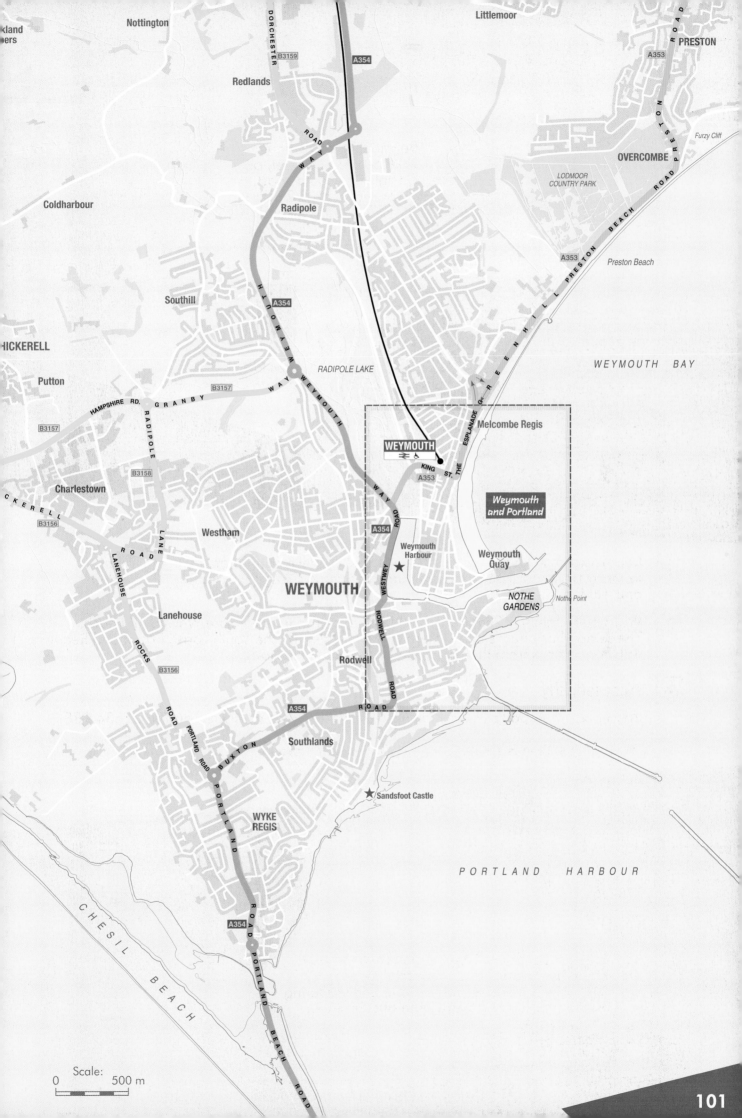

Nottington

Littlemoor

PRESTON

Redlands

A354

A353

DORCHESTER

B3159

A354

Furzy Cliff

Coldharbour

Radipole

OVERCOMBE

LODMOOR
COUNTRY PARK

Southill

A354

ROAD

PRESTON

WEYMOUTH

GREEN HILL

PRESTON BEACH

WEYMOUTH BAY

RADIPOLE LAKE

A353

Preston Beach

HICKERELL

HAMPSHIRE RD.

B3157

GRANBY

WAY

Putton

B3157

WEYMOUTH

ESPLANADE

Melcombe Regis

RADIPOLE

B3158

WEYMOUTH

Weymouth
and Portland

Charlestown

KING ST.

THE

A353

CKERELL

B3156

ROAD

LANE

Westham

A354

ROAD

Weymouth Harbour

Weymouth
Quay

B3156

ROAD

LANEHOUSE

WEYMOUTH

WESTWEY

★

NOTHE
GARDENS

Nothe Point

Lanehouse

RODWELL

ROCKS

B3156

Rodwell

ROAD

ROAD

Southlands

A354

ROAD

PORTLAND ROAD

BUXTON

PORTLAND

WYKE
REGIS

★ Sandsfoot Castle

PORTLAND HARBOUR

CHESIL

A354

ROAD

PORTLAND

BEACH

ROAD

Scale:

0   500 m

CHESIL BEACH

101

Weymouth and Portland
29 July - 11 August

1 - 6 September

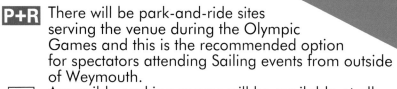

Getting to the Venue

P+R There will be park-and-ride sites serving the venue during the Olympic Games and this is the recommended option for spectators attending Sailing events from outside of Weymouth.

♿ Accessible parking spaces will be available at all parking sites with shuttles to the venue which are suitable for a wide range of disabled spectators including wheelchair users.

🚌 For the Olympic Games, there will be 2012 Games coach services to Preston Beach from a range of locations within Great Britain. Services are planned to arrive at the venue for the start of sessions.

🚌 There is a good local bus network in the Weymouth area, with plenty of routes and stops close to the venue and other good vantage points to watch the competitions.

🚶 There is a network of walking routes in and around Weymouth that provide good access to the venue. There are also some spectacular coastal walks providing good vantage points to view the Sailing competitions. There will also be a park-and-walk site approximately 40 minutes walk from the ticketed venue.

🚲P There is a network of cycling routes in and around Weymouth. The venue is located on the National Cycle Network route 26, which runs from Portland Bill to Weymouth and on to Dorchester. Free, secure, managed cycle parking will be provided at the venue.

🚕 The main taxi rank will be at the Park Street car park in Weymouth town centre.

♿P Limited, pre-booked parking will be provided close to the venue for disabled spectators who are UK Blue Badge holders or members of an equivalent national scheme.

Scan for the latest transport information

•••• Recommended spectator access routes to and from the venue.

🚶 Venue entrance or exit.

 London 2012 Live Site, Weymouth beach.

Sailing

Led by triple gold medal-winner Ben Ainslie CBE, Team GB has topped the Sailing medals table at the last three Olympic Games.

The 10 different Olympic Sailing events (6 for men, 4 for women) will feature a variety of craft, from dinghies and keelboats to windsurfing boards.

Sailing

The yachts used in Paralympic Sailing have keels, mainly because the design provides greater stability. These keelboats also have open cockpits to allow more room for the sailors.

RADIPOLE LAKE
(Nature Reserve
and Swannery)

RSPB
Centre

P+R

A354

TSBURY

RANELAGH

PARK

RADIPOLE

JUBILEE RETAIL
PARK

WEYMOUTH ♿

KING STREET

BRIDGE

COMMERCIAL

ROAD

A353

SWANNERY

DRIVE

A354

WESTWAY ROAD

RODWELL

XTON ROAD

RODWELL ROAD

A354

Rodwell

AVENUE SPRING ROAD

RODWELL

STREET

QUEEN STREET

BATH ST.

GLOUCESTER STREET

TURTON ST.

WOOP-
ERTON
ST.

PARK STREET

GLOUCESTER STREET

MEWS

THE ESPLANADE

ESPLANADE A353

GREEN HILL

Melcombe
Regis

WEYMOUTH BAY

WESTHAM ROAD

WESTHAM ROAD

GEORGE STREET

GREAT GEORGE STREET

SCH. ST.

Library

NEW BOND ST.
& COLWELL
SHOPPING CENTRES

NEW
BOND ST.

BOND STREET

ST. THOMAS STREET

ST. ALBAN STREET

Cineworld

LOWER ST. ALBAN ST.

ST. ALBAN ST.

THE ESPLANADE

WEYMOUTH

LS

Weymouth
& Portland

Weymouth
Quay

The Weymouth
Tower

Pleasure
Pier

Commercial
Pier

Ferry
Terminal

South
Pier

Pavilion
Theatre

Ferry
(Foot)

Nothe
Fort

Nothe Point

NOTHE GARDENS

ROAD

Newton's Cove

PORTLAND HARBOUR

Scale:
0   100 m

LWR.
ST. EDMUND ST.

ST. THOMAS ST.

ST. EDMUND
ST.

COMMERCIAL ROAD

WEYMOUTH
HARBOUR

sh
.

Courts

rstore ROAD

Fire
Sta.

NORTH

Council
Offices

QUAY

CUSTOM

TRINITY

† TRINITY ROAD

COVE ROW

COVE

TRINITY ST.

HOUSE QUAY

ESPLANADE

PARADE

Lifeboat
Station

🚶

🚶

ADMIRALS
QUARTER

🚲 P

LOOK
OUT

BARRACK ROAD

NOTHE ST.

ST. NOTHE

SPRING ST.

HOPE ST.

HILL LA.

RD.

HORSFORD ST.

103

Sailor Ben Ainslie of Great Britain
leads the medal race in the Finn class
2008 Beijing Olympic Games

Picture Credits:

© Getty Images: 37, 48, 78, 102, 104

© ODA: 2, 3, 14, 20-23, 26 (1.), 32, 56, 60, 66 (1.), 82, 86, 98, Back cover

© www.Bigstock.com: 26 (2.), 28 (1.), 40, 42, 44, 46, 50 (3.), 58, 62 (3.), 64,
70 (2.), 72 (2.3.), 74, 76, 80, 84 (2.), 88 (1.2.), 92, 94, 96 (1.), 100

© A-Z Maps: 28 (2.), 34, 50 (1.), 52, 62 (1.), 70 (3.)

© www.iStockphoto.com: 30, 54, 66 (3.), 84 (1.), 88 (3.), 90

© www.Shutterstock.com: 50 (2.), 62 (2.), 66 (2.4.), 68, 70 (1.), 72 (1.), 96 (2.)